DON'T DROP YOUR KIDS OFF AT CHURCH

DON'T DROP YOUR KIDS OFF AT CHURCH
BRING THEM HOME TO IT

TRAVIS AGNEW
travisagnew.org

TAG PUBLISHING

Don't Drop Your Kids Off at Church
Copyright © 20011 by Travis B. Agnew
Tag Publishing
All rights reserved.
Printed in the United States of America

ISBN-13:   978-1466320291
ISBN-10:   146632029X

Scripture quotations are from The Holy Bible, English Standard Version®, copyright © 2001 by Crossway Bibles, a publishing ministry of Good News Publishers. Used by permission. All rights reserved.

All rights reserved. No part of this publication may be reproduced, stored, in a retrieval system, or transmitted in any form or by any means -- electronic, mechanical, photocopy, recording, or any other -- except for brief quotations in printed reviews, without the prior permission of the publisher.

Printed in the United States of America.

To OBADIAH & ELI,

May the fruit of this work
further equip you to be true worshipers
of Yahweh all of your days.

CONTENTS

| 1 | YOUR CHILD'S BEST CHANCE | 21 |

SECTION 1: THE BIBLICAL MANDATE

2	GOD'S CALL ON A PARENT'S LIFE	39
3	THE LOVE OF YOUR LIFE	53
4	AS FOR ME AND MY HOUSE	67
5	GENERATIONAL HAND-ME DOWNS	81
6	THE IMPORTANCE OF FATHERS	93
7	A LESS-THAN-IDEAL HOME	107

SECTION 2: THE EFFECTIVE METHODS

8	GOSPEL ESSENTIALS	125
9	LEVELS OF LEARNING	139
10	CHILD STEPS	153

SECTION 3: THE HEALTHY UNION

11	THE PARADIGM SHIFT	173
12	THE FAMILY ALTAR	187
13	EQUIPPING PARENTS	201

APPENDIX

1	MINISTRY OUTLINE	219
2	CROSSROADS OUTLINE	247
3	PROJECT DEVOTIONAL GUIDE	251
4	GRACE OUTLINE	259
5	FOCUS GROUP QUESTIONNAIRE	263
6	LEGACY OUTLINE	267
7	MAKING FAITH STICK OUTLINE	273
8	MAKING FAITH STICK EVALUATION	287
9	PROJECT GOALS	291
	BIBLIOGRAPHY	299

PREFACE

As I made the final adjustments to this book, I was humbly reminded of all the people God used to help me finish. Working closely with Chuck Lawless was an academic privilege and a spiritual blessing as he pushed me forward in both areas. Jeff Walters and the staff at the Billy Graham School of Missions and Evangelism at the Southern Baptist Theological Seminary always made themselves available to assist me in this process.

I am also indebted to Pastor Jeff Lethco, the leadership, and the people at North Side Baptist Church in Greenwood, South Carolina. Many people told me not to work at the church where I was raised, but I am thankful that this partnership has been fruitful in my life and, I pray, in theirs. I gratefully thank North Side for making loving God and loving people a reality in the context of a local church. As I turned this academic work into a more accessible read, I am also indebted to Cheryl Bell, Tara Harris, Heather Kennerly, Angela McCall, John McFadden, and Jessica Wolfe for their editing work.

God has also placed numerous encouraging voices in my life. From loving parents, family members, in-laws, and friends, so many of them have helped motivate me to finish and finish well. Through their encouraging spirits, prayerful hearts, and willing minds, we have walked through this journey together.

I also would like to thank Obadiah Benjamin and Eli Botela, our sons, for being born. When God brought them into this world, everything changed – including the focus of this project. Their presence in this world makes me redefine success and makes me want to be a better father over being a more prominent minister or scholar any day. I love being their dad.

When my wife, Amanda, encouraged me to begin this degree, I am not positive she or I knew what all it would entail. Along the way, I made her promise that this project would never come before our family, and I thank her for always keeping that in check. I am the most blessed man alive because of her. I would follow Jesus all by myself if that were his call on my life, but I am profoundly glad he has let me follow with Amanda by my side. I never knew I could love someone this much or be loved by someone so much. The best is yet to come.

Finally, I saved the best for last – Jesus. He is still my favorite. Being redeemed by his grace in my sin was immeasurably more than I ever deserved (Rom 5:8), but he has allowed me to be a friend (John 15:14-15) and an ambassador (2 Cor 5:20). All of life is by him and all of mine is still for him (Col 1:16).

Travis B. Agnew
Greenwood, South Carolina
October 2011

CHAPTER 1
YOUR CHILD'S BEST CHANCE

On May 6, 2008, everything changed for me. As I stood in Self Regional Hospital in Greenwood, South Carolina and the doctor handed my firstborn, Obadiah, to me, I knew that nothing would ever be the same. As I began to sing the song I had sung to him over and over in the womb, he calmed down just long enough to lock eyes with me: "You and I are made to worship."

We decided to name him Obadiah because it meant "worshiper of Yahweh" or "servant of the LORD." I couldn't think of a better way to describe how I wanted his life to be characterized. I wanted him to see his entire life as an expression of worship to God. After many prayers and nine months of anticipation, he was finally in my arms.

I will never forget that pivotal moment in my life. Right then, I experienced overwhelming joy, and at the same time, unbelievable responsibility. God had given me a baby boy that he was calling me to raise and nurture. I felt more than unqualified — I was terrified. I did not want Obadiah to miss God's best because I could not fulfill my God-given role.

During that summer, the time also came for me to declare my focus for my doctoral project at The Southern Baptist Theological Seminary. The focus of this evangelism and church growth project was supposed to be something that would stretch me as a student and benefit my church at the same time. Most of the declared emphases centered around ministry-focused outreach efforts.

As I prayed for my specific direction, Obadiah kept coming to my mind. I felt a burden for the children of my church, North Side Baptist, as well. Beyond our church context, I was also noticing alarming cultural trends. It seemed like our ministry efforts in America for the next generation were more polished than ever before and yet we were simply losing that generation. For all the underage in church attendance, change seemed only temporary for the very few taking seriously the claims of Christ. Throughout America, many churches had more bells and whistles than at any other time, and yet we were experiencing minimal success.

During my time of prayer and study, the direction became clear. The focus of my study was going to be on how to equip parents to evangelize and disciple their children. I could not imagine anything with a greater possibility to change our church than if our parents saw it as their God-given responsibility to make disciples out of the next generation.

I didn't want to "write the book" after I had raised my child. I wanted to prepare the best that I could to give Obadiah the best chance at following Christ. At that time, I was witnessing things in our church that were alarming me. The longer I invested into the programs of our local church, the more I saw many disturbing trends which were enabling parents to be passive in their children's spiritual formation. When I declared the project's focus, I already had numerous rationales in my mind of why this was not only important for my family and my church, but for many others as well.

RATIONALE

The first rationale for this project was that the Bible commands parents to evangelize and disciple their children. The scriptural mandate, indicated throughout the entire Bible, for a child's spiritual development is unashamedly centered around the home.[1] The New Testament church saw fathers' leading the home spiritually as so important that if a father did not fulfill his parental responsibility, he was unfit for church leadership positions (1 Tim 3:4-5).

For some parents, the problem is not they do not know how to invest in their children spiritually; they simply do not see that act as a priority. Most American parents view children's spiritual development as a positive element in child rearing, but they do not see it as the most important element.[2] Parents have often developed misplaced priorities when it comes to their children. Many children in America are so busy with numerous activities that their spiritual lives are neglected.

While it is a lofty goal for a child to receive a great education or to have a financially secure life, that ambition is not God's most important goal for parents. If God views children as a gift to parents (Ps 127:3), then parents need to conform their perspective of parenting to God's perspective.[3] Voddie Baucham stated, "There are many worthwhile pursuits in this world, but few of them rise to the level of training our children to follow the Lord and keep his commandments."[4]

God left no room for misunderstanding in the area of parental responsibility.[5] Parents are required to teach the children to love God (Deut 6:4-9), and they are expected to teach them that truth in every arena in life (Deut 11:18-21). A parent ought to teach children to love God more than they love their own parents (Matt 10:37). Solomon exhorted that a well instructed child would not likely depart from the teaching of his or her parents (Prov 22:6). Through these examples and more, the Bible is clear in revealing God's heart that parents have the responsibility to raise their children spiritually.

The second rationale behind this project was that churches must address the fact that many children raised in the church are walking away from that institution once they leave home. For most congregations, the significant investment towards children and youth is providing a minimal return. While these students are active in church when they are at home due to sincere desire or parental prodding, once they leave home for college, churches will lose a large percentage of these students.[6]

Although the research varies slightly, most records indicate that between 70 and 88 percent of Christian students are absent from the local church by the time they enter their second year of college.[7] Those numbers scream that something is missing. Every dollar spent on nursery cribs to youth trips to graduation Bibles seems to be in vain when students apparently vanish from church for years after high school graduation.

Many students stop growing in Christ because a walk with Christ is not witnessed in the home. Instead of modeling that type of relationship with God, parents hope that by bringing their children to church, someone else will take care of their children's spiritual health. If that is the sole parental input into a child's spiritual development, a child will experience great spiritual struggles once he or she leaves the home.

> Many students stop growing in Christ because a walk with Christ is not witnessed in the home.

In 2003, the Barna Group conducted extensive research on the children of America. From this study, this group discovered that 91 percent of 13-year-olds pray to God at least once a week, 61 percent attend weekly worship services, and 45 percent read their Bible on their own outside of a church context.[8] While the statistics seem encouraging, those religious activities do not magically produce disciples. For all of this church activity, 75 percent of those students believe that someone can gain entrance into heaven by simply doing good works.[9]

Bringing children to church will not save them. While parents ought to bring children to church functions, the probability of children remaining involved in a church once they leave home based upon mere church exposure once or twice a week during childhood is minimal.[10]

Many children in America are so busy with activities in academics, athletics, or some other endeavor that their spiritual lives are not valued or prioritized.[11]

A third rationale behind this project was that, in order to ensure the greatest success, parents and the local church must partner together to evangelize and disciple the children. If parents are to teach their children the ways of the Lord, they must be intentional about bringing spirituality into their conversations.[12] Some parents, upon realization of the biblical mandate for parenting, are too guilty to admit they have neglected spiritual conversations in the home and are too ashamed to make the needed change in their homes.[13] Unfortunately, multiple families are simply too disinterested in making Christ the center of their homes.[14]

Many parents passively expect the church to do all the work associated with their children's spiritual upbringing.[15] Parents' general attitude towards their involvement normally consists of connecting their children with the most qualified professionals leading the most appealing programs and then stepping out of the professionals' way. How can parents safely assume that another person will have as much concern about their child's salvation as they will themselves? Due to seemingly sufficient children programming in churches, parents have eased into complacency regarding their children's spiritual development.[16] Nevertheless, a church staff and the children's parents must agree upon a biblical, healthy partnership to give each child the best opportunity to follow Christ.[17]

Additionally, many de-churched young adults have lost contact with their spiritual mentors from youth.

In light of the high turnover rate of pastoral staffs in churches, many of these spiritual mentors for young people are replaced within a short amount of time causing a lack in consistent spiritual leadership. Plus, once one group graduates, a new group of students take their place and require the student pastor's limited time and attention.

Many college students were involved in church, especially their youth group, in middle school and high school. Once they got away from home, however, they stopped growing in Christ and connecting to a church. If a relationship with God had been mentored by a student's parents and not merely a church staff member, the student would continue to have access to his or her mentors once in college.

The final rationale of this project was purely personal. Because of my experience of being raised in a home affected by divorce, I desired to put Christ in the center of my adult home so that my children could benefit from what I did not receive in the fullest sense. While I am truly grateful to God for providing me with loving parents and countless people sent my way who would impact me for Christ, I started my spiritual pilgrimage at a slight disadvantage.

Complaining about my personal circumstances is superfluous for my life now, but I can use my situation as a stimulus to provide the best opportunity for my children to love God with all their heart, soul, and might (Deut 6:5). If I take seriously God's commands concerning my parental responsibility, my children and the generations to follow will be blessed by my faithfulness (Exod 20:5-6). With the birth of our first child, my earnest desire was to focus my heart, my resources, and my effort to raise our son and any children that might follow him in a home that not only teaches that Christ is first but also shows him that Christ is first. Through the work of this project, I intended to equip myself with the tools needed to effectively share the gospel with my own children and make disciples of them by teaching them to obey everything Jesus has commanded us (Matt 28:18-20).

WHERE TO START

My favorite part of my day is playing outside with my boys in the evening. While the sun begins to set, we ride cars, push wagons, and play ball. After we have sweated and gotten ourselves completely out of breath, we usually eat a popsicle and get ready for bath time.

When we were teaching the boys to throw and kick the ball, something unique happened one evening in the front yard. I kept attempting to share the ball with the boys, but their favorite thing was not to have the ball themselves. They wanted Dad to have it.

"Daddy, kick the ball high?" Unwilling to disappoint, I would kick the ball as high as I could. They would run and chase the ball down and bring it right back to me.

"Daddy, kick the ball high?"

"Thanks, buddy, but why don't you kick the ball? Here you go."

"Daddy, kick the ball high?"

I kicked that red ball all night long. They knew they were able to kick it, but they also knew that Dad could kick it higher. For whatever reason, watching their father kick it higher was better than them kicking it themselves.

Something exists in the heart of children to watch their parents do what they cannot do yet. They stand in awe at early ages of what their parents can do. While my ability to kick a ball high may be impressive, I desperately want my children to stand in awe of the way I live for God. I don't care if they are impressed by the house in which we live, the details of our vacation spots, or the hobbies that I master. I want them to see me living for Christ all of their days. When asked about their greatest spiritual mentors, I pray that they model after the ministers in our church, but how I deeply want to make that list as well. Could I live in such a way that my children would know what it means to follow Christ if no one else taught them but me? Can I model obedience to God rather than just mentioning its importance?

This world is a challenging place for a child to become a disciple of Jesus Christ. The solution is not the hippest youth minister in town, the most alluring programs, or the church gymnasium where all the cool kids hang out. The solution for your children is you. Children need their parents to invest spiritually in their lives. We need to be the ones telling them the gospel. We need to be the ones modeling what it looks like to live for Christ. Our lives should be the greatest sermon they ever hear.

If that idea is intimidating to you, I promise that you are not alone. Every honest parent would admit that evangelizing and discipling one's children is a daunting task. While the challenge is great, disciples are known by their willingness to risk everything and be used by God in what seems improbable or even impossible.

You have a limited window of time with your children in their formative years. How will you spend it? You may be an empty-nester who has a list of regrets longer than your list of approved accomplishments, but it is not too late to make an impact on your children. We all are leaving a legacy, but it has yet to be declared what each of ours will be.

No one leaves a godly legacy by accident. Throughout this process, God revealed biblical principles and parental practices that are being used to make disciples of the next generation. I watched God use his Word to impact my home and my church, and faithful stewardship beckons me to share with you what he taught us during this process.

> No one leaves a godly legacy by accident.

In the following pages, I have attempted to make this information palatable for both pastors and parents. I will present research findings and personal testimonies of what happens when parents raise kids with the Kingdom in mind. Hopefully, the impact will be felt for generations to come. As one generation of parents evangelizes and disciples their children, countless generations in your family and in your church could be changed.

In the first section of this book, we will look at the biblical mandate. These biblical passages are often overlooked but possess key principles for parents of every generation. In the second section, we will study the effective methods of parents who are evangelizing and discipling their children. This section gives practical help to sharing the gospel with one's children and dealing with issues such as the age of accountability. In the final section, we will discover that a healthy union between the home and the church can exist. Simple changes could be made to every church which would enable church staffs and programs to assist and support parents as they evangelize and disciple their children, and not vice versa.

    I have also included an appendix full of series outlines, course outlines, ministry processes, and much more. Since I had to chronicle all my steps to this process, I thought it would be helpful stewardship to include in this volume. I pray that the information can help equip you to evangelize and disciple your children.

    At the time of this writing, I have two toddlers and one more on the way. Rest assured, the following content is not full of stories concerning how I have been successful. I will be presenting foundational truths from God's Word. I will be sharing my findings on what is working with successful parents. My goal is to equip you as a parent to be the primary evangelist and disciple-maker of your children.

    In American culture, we have often confused a the local church with a building. In the Greek language, the word "church" literally meant "group" or "assembly." When Jesus set out to build his church, he spoke of one big family that prized the Kingdom of God more than anything else.

    So, let me assure you: the church is vital to your child's spiritual upbringing, but the buildings and the programs are not the church Jesus had in mind. If there are believers in your home, then an important part of the church of Jesus Christ resides in your home. As parents, we must stop idly expecting someone else to do what God has commanded us to do. Don't drop your kids off at church — bring them home to it.

---

[1] Donald Whitney, Family Worship: In the Bible, in History and in Your Home (Shepherdsville, KY: The Center of Biblical Spirituality, 2005), 11.

[2] George Barna, Transforming Children into Spiritual Champions (Ventura, CA: Regal, 2003), 14.

[3] Ibid., 44.

[4] Voddie Baucham, Family Driven Faith: Doing What It Takes to Raise Sons and Daughters Who Walk with God (Wheaton, IL: Crossway Books, 2007), 29.

[5] Barna, Transforming Children, 82.

[6] Baucham, Family Driven Faith, 7.

[7] Ibid., 10.

[8] Barna, Transforming Children, 35.

[9] Ibid., 36.

[10] Whitney, Family Worship, 8.

[11] Barna, Transforming Children, 29.

[12] Whitney, Family Worship, 15.

[13] Ibid., 48.

[14] Ibid., 54.

[15] Ibid., 8.

[16] Baucham, Family Driven Faith, 12.

[17] Ibid., 14.

# SECTION 1:
THE BIBLICAL MANDATE
WHAT HAPPENS WHEN GOD'S WORD INVADES YOUR HOME

1

CHAPTER 2
GOD'S CALL ON A PARENT'S LIFE

I'll never forget the look in Brian's eyes. My pastor and I had just tag-team preached a message on the biblical role of parents. God was working in our hearts concerning how families and our church intersected, and we took the last Sunday of the year to cast a vision of what could happen if parents took God's Word seriously in the area of parenthood.

He grabbed me after the service and said, "I get it. I buy the concept completely. I truly desire to disciple my children, but honestly, Trav, I have no idea where to start."

Neither did I. At that point, we had merely exposed the need and directed our congregation towards one passage of Scripture. My plan was simply to challenge our church that morning. People were eager to begin, and we had to figure out how to lead them forward. We were unsure what this would look like in the months to come. Confident that God was giving us a direction, we had yet to discover the map.

So I began to study God's Word concerning parenting. The Bible is full of parental expectations, but in our culture, it is often overlooked because it is not written in bulleted lists contained in a parenting magazine. The Bible specializes in parenting principles rather than practices. God didn't provide itemized lists probably because the practice would shift somewhat from generation to generation. Fortunately, the principles are there and God's instructions provide more than an adequate framework in order to reorient our homes.

For the task of evangelizing and discipling your children, parental responsibility is not a novel concept – the task is a biblical mandate. God chose Israel in the Old Testament (Gen 17:4) and the church in the New Testament (Matt 16:18) to be his chosen body, and the institution of the family has always maintained a critical role in God's plan. For parents to become the primary evangelists and disciple-makers in their children's lives, they must comprehend that critical biblical mandate for the sake of future generations. God's Word is full of biblical passages which reveal parental responsibility concerning the spiritual nurturing of children. Parental spiritual responsibility is not an isolated thought by certain biblical writers, but a recurring theme of the entire Bible.

OLD TESTAMENT TEACHINGS

Biblical authors filled the Old Testament pages with stories about families. Many of the family narratives reveal that God placed a high priority on the institution of the home. Unfortunately, the families of the Book of Genesis alone reveal a faithless record, with key family leaders failing to fulfill their familial roles (Gen 3:12), killing one's own brother (Gen 4:8), becoming shamefully drunk (Gen 9:21), abandoning one's own wife (Gen 12:13), encouraging one's spouse to commit adultery (Gen 16:2), deceiving family members for the sake of birthrights (Gen 27:5-10), selling one's brother into slavery (Gen 37:27-28), and even engaging in sex with one's daughter-in-law (Gen 38:16). And you thought your family had issues!

The families of the Old Testament did not typically live up to their calling. Throughout these unfortunate events, God spoke directly or through a messenger to remind the people concerning his unwavering dedication to families. In these Old Testament passages, God required parents to assume responsibility for their children's development, to model unwavering love for the Lord, to choose to serve the Lord above other gods, and to remember God's faithfulness to a faithless people. In one pivotal passage concerning Abraham, the father of Israel, God reveals his expected parental responsibilities.

UNDERSTANDING PARENTAL RESPONSIBILITIES

Genesis 18:16 Then the men set out from there, and they looked down toward Sodom. And Abraham went with them to set them on their way. 17 The LORD said, "Shall I hide from Abraham what I am about to do, 18 seeing that Abraham shall surely become a great and mighty nation, and all the nations of the earth shall be blessed in him?

19 For I have chosen him, that he may command his children and his household after him to keep the way of the LORD by doing righteousness and justice, so that the LORD may bring to Abraham what he has promised him." 20 Then the LORD said, "Because the outcry against Sodom and Gomorrah is great and their sin is very grace, 21 I will go down to see whether they have done altogether according to the outcry that has come to me. And if not, I will know."

The author of Genesis describes Sodom's destruction in Genesis 18:16-19:29.[1] Three divine guests visit Abraham, the father of Israel, before they travel to Sodom to survey the exceedingly sinful city. Some scholars believe that the three men should be understood as Yahweh (the Hebrew covenantal name for the Lord) accompanied by two "members of the divine council (Jer 23:18)."[2]

Instead of sitting with his guests to eat, Abraham stood near them, which was not common practice for a host during this time. These guests inquired about Sarah's whereabouts, for she was waiting in the part of the tent designated for females because women were forbidden to eat with the men.[3] While Abraham had previously heard Yahweh's promise of a child and laughed at the absurd idea due to his and Sarah's ages (Gen 17:16-17), this encounter was Sarah's first chance to hear for herself the improbable news as she eavesdropped upon their conversation (Gen 18:10).[4]

After the three men explained that Sarah would give birth to a child and the accompanying laughing ensued, the men began to look toward Sodom. This glancing toward the city serves as "an ominous tone that hints at what is to come."[5] It was not necessary for Yahweh to behold Sodom's sinfulness in person (Gen 18:21), but he was using this moment before Sodom's judgment as an opportunity to descend upon the earth physically in order to apprise Abraham as a father since Abraham would in turn instruct God's nation in a fatherly manner.[6]

As a good host, Abraham escorted his guests for some distance on the next part of their journey. As they continued to travel toward Sodom, Abraham realized that this mission was leading toward the city where his nephew, Lot, and his family lived.[7] When God questioned whether or not he should conceal information from Abraham, he was apparently not speaking concerning the future destruction of Sodom; rather, God was speaking concerning the desired future of Abraham and his family.[8]

At this point in the narrative, God reiterated to the angelic beings that he had specifically chosen Abraham to start his nation. Yahweh used the word *yada* to describe his relationship with Abraham. Through the use of the word *yada*, Yahweh indicated that he had "an intimate relationship" with Abraham.[9] While Abraham understood that God had chosen him before this encounter, Yahweh further revealed the purpose for which Abraham had been chosen. Yahweh purposed Abraham to develop a community of Yahweh followers. Before the nations could be blessed, Abraham would have to instill obedience into the lives of his very own family.[10]

God desired Abraham to comprehend the destruction of Sodom in order to impress a warning concerning the penalties of sin upon the following generations.[11] If the upcoming Hebrew nation were to understand God's justice, the nation's father must understand that concept first.[12] Not only did God desire to reveal his plans to Abraham due to his election, but God also desired to educate Abraham for his family's sake.[13]

What happens next almost seems out of context. As God has conversed concerning the leveling of sinful cities, appointment of chosen nations, and circumstances with global implications, he explains Abraham's task. It almost appears to be too trivial and too small of a thing in light of the prior discussion.

"Shall I hide from Abraham what I am about to do, seeing that Abraham shall surely become a great and mighty nation, and all the nations of the earth shall be blessed in him? For I have chosen him, that he may command his children and his household after him to keep the way of the Lord by doing righteousness and justice, so that the Lord may bring to Abraham what he has promised him" (Gen 18:17-19).

God's global plan of redemption, his strategy to bless all the nations of the world, began with one father teaching his one family to keep the way of the Lord. Simplistic? Yes. Effective? Absolutely. God did not say the first step was for Abraham to perform miraculous feats to bring the mightiest kings to their knees. His first task was not to align a military powerhouse that would level the pagan nations. His first task was not to erect a grandiose religious temple where followers could worship. His first task was to have a child and teach that child everything he knew about following God.

Abraham's role in blessing all the families of the world was directly related to the fulfillment in his role as a husband and father.[14] God gave Abraham the chance to live out his purpose of teaching the future generations since he lived for sixty years of his son Issac's life and the first fifteen years of the lives of his twin grandsons, Jacob and Esau. Yahweh's plan was for this nation to impress its spiritual heritage upon following generations through the home (Deut 6:6; Prov 1:8), and Yahweh impressed this notion upon Abraham (Gen 18:19) even before his promised son was born (Gen 21:2-3).[15]

God intended Abraham to instruct his family to live righteously in order to make the families of the world righteous.[16] While Abraham had a global mission, his first step in seeing that purpose succeed was to teach his children. Before Abraham would be a leader of a people, he would be a leader of a home. Yahweh's instruction to the father of the Hebrews serves as a reminder to all followers of Yahweh that one of the most important tasks of any father is to teach the succeeding generations the way of the Lord. As fathers teach children spiritual truth, each family can serve as a witness to reach other families far from God.

It is easy for parents and churches to get off this track. All sincere parties involved in your child's spiritual formation deeply desire legitimate conversion and growth. Unfortunately, we expect that God must use complex approaches to get the task done. Much in the way we expect God to commission Abraham with some corporate task, we also expect God to give us instructions on a larger scale. I can prove it. Does your church focus more time on developing programs on a church campus for your child or developing you as parents to go to your home and disciple your child?

What was the last uproar about in your church's children's or youth ministry? Was it about an ineffective program? Was it concern about teenagers not wanting to come on Wednesday nights? Was it disapproval of how a church staff was programming events for someone's kids? Or was it a desperate parent asking for help in discipling their children?

I imagine that most of the triumphs and tragedies concerning your child's spiritual formation are centered around organized church activity and not intentional family life. The problem is God never intended organized religion to replace the family. God did not expect Abraham to rally a nation of God's people together to invest in his child; he expected Abraham to assume that blessed responsibility himself. It was Abraham's job. God had given that task to him specifically.

> The problem is God never intended organized religion to replace the family.

Before Abraham even had a son, God allowed for no speculation concerning his parental responsibilities. God expected Abraham to "command his children and his household after him to keep the way of the Lord by doing righteousness and justice" (Gen. 18:19). He was to direct them to faithful devotion to the one true God. He was expected to do it by modeling righteousness and justice before their very eyes.

SUCCESSFUL PARENTING

LifeWay Research conducted a national survey of 1,200 adults with children under 18 at home. They attempted to discover what parents in America defined as "successful parenting." Their findings were interesting yet not shocking. 25% of those interviewed would view their jobs as parents as successful if their children were happy as adults. 22% were hoping their children would find success in adulthood. Another 17% defined success when a child graduated from college. Only 9% of those surveyed view their job to produce godly children.

What was enlightening about this study is that 82% of those parents polled were fearful concerning the state of the world their children would inherit. With such a vast majority concerned about the future, only 14% of those parents were aware of what the Bible says concerning parenting.[17] Genesis 18 leaves no room for guesswork. God defines successful parenting as commanding one's children "to keep the way of the LORD by doing righteousness and justice" (Gen. 18:19). Any other parental pursuit is insignificant to this original command, and any attempted handoff of one's children is cheating them of God's ideal.

During a car ride one particular evening, I asked the boys to tell me what their favorite part of the day was. My second child, Eli, loudly proclaimed, "Jonah and the fish!" Their mother had attended a Bible study that morning and took the boys to the daycare program provided by the organization. These dedicated workers did more than provide Goldfish snacks and wet wipes — they always taught the children a Bible story in a memorable way.

As the boys began to retell this Bible story to me in a uniquely humorous fashion, I suddenly realized what had happened and became very upset. Someone else had the privilege of telling my boys that story before I did. We had read biblical stories, but I had not taught them this specific story yet. I was outraged! How dare this mini-van driving, Veggie Tales watching, multitasking, soccer mom tell my boys about Jonah? That was my job!

Unfortunately, this woman of God who saw my boys once a week, as a volunteer, had gotten around to it before their dad who lived in the home with them had made the time. That night reminded me of my task to teach my children the truths of God's Word. I could never run out of material to teach my boys concerning the glorious deeds of our God! While they sat in the backseat of my truck, I started at Genesis 1, and by the time we pulled into the driveway, we were rounding the corner into Joshua! Parents, it is our job to tell our children the great and wonderful acts of our loving and powerful Lord.

When an additional voice teaches our children about the Bible, it should serve as a reinforcement and not as an introduction. When our lives back up the biblical truths we teach them, impact occurs. An integral part of God's global plan of redemption has always been parents teaching their children the ways of the LORD.

> The most critical spiritual environment is the one in which you live.

The most critical spiritual environment is the one in which you live. No weekly programs can compare to the impact of consistent, intentional parents. Don't expect anyone to have impact on your children than you will if you maintain righteousness and justice before their eyes.

---

[1] Gordon J. Wenham, Genesis 16-50, Word Biblical Commentary, vol. 2 (Dallas: Word, 1994), 49.

[2] Ibid., 50.

[3] Howard Frederic Vos, Genesis (Chicago: Moody, 1982), 76.

[4] Ronald F. Youngblood, The Book of Genesis: An Introductory Commentary (Grand Rapids: Baker, 1991), 174.

[5] Bill T. Arnold, Encountering the Book of Genesis, Encountering Biblical Studies (Grand Rapids: Baker, 1998), 102.

[6] John H. Walton, Genesis: From Biblical Text...to Contemporary Life, The NIV Application Commentary (Grand Rapids: Zondervan, 2001), 475.

[7] Joyce G. Baldwin, The Message of Genesis 12-50: From Abraham to Joseph, The Bible Speaks Today (Leicester, England: InterVarsity, 1986), 73.

[8] Victor P. Hamilton, The Book of Genesis: Chapters 18-50, The New International Commentary on the Old Testament (Grand Rapids: Eerdmans, 1995), 17.

[9] Bruce K. Waltke and Cathi J. Fredricks, Genesis: A Commentary (Grand Rapids: Zondervan, 2001), 268.

[10] Wenham, Genesis 16-50, 50.

[11] Vos, Genesis, 76.

[12] Waltke and Fredericks, Genesis, 269.

[13] K. A. Mathews, Genesis 11:27-50:26, The New American Commentary, vol. 1B (Nashville: Broadman and Holman, 2005), 223.

[14] Hamilton, The Book of Genesis, 19.

[15] Waltke and Fredericks, Genesis, 269.

[16] Mathews, Genesis 11:27-50:26, 223.

[17] Mark Kelly, "LifeWay Research finds parents look inward not upward for guidance," accessed 9 September 2011 [on-line]; http://www.lifeway.com/Article/LifeWay-Research-finds-parents-look-inward-not-upward-for-guidance.

CHAPTER 3
THE LOVE OF YOUR LIFE

     One Saturday morning, I attempted to break the world record for how much yard work one man could do in one day. I had finished trimming, edging, mulching, and I was finally nearing completion as I began to ride the lawnmower. I was nasty, tired, and singing along to some Fred Hammond on the iPod when I caught a glimpse of something that absolutely made my day.

     A couple of 2-year-old boys were moving in our front window with their heads pressed up against the glass watching me. As I went side to side through the yard, their little eyes followed me everywhere the mower would take me. They would knock on the window if I wasn't supplying enough silly faces to make them laugh. They would wave at me to make sure I saw them when I got far away. Every move I made, they followed.

     In that moment, they were mesmerized with their daddy. As I finished cutting the front yard, I teared up a bit (because you can't cry on a lawn mower — it's not allowed). As I watched these precious sons of mine and their unwavering devotion to my movement, I realized what a unique stage of life I was living at that time. Many people told me that there is a limited time in which I would be my sons' hero. While part of me understood that and agreed completely, a part of me wanted to buck that trend. Why couldn't I be my sons' hero for the rest of their lives? What if I lived in such a way that they were mesmerized by more than just my mowing capabilities?

At age 2, my boys were watching my every move, and they were learning much about their father. They could comprehend what made me joyful. They had seen what would cause me to lose my temper. Additionally, they were aware of what truly had captured their father's heart.

I believe children of every age know what it is that their parents love. Whether it's somebody or something, our words and our actions declare those things that have our hearts. They are observant enough to see what it is that wakes us up in the morning and lingers on our minds until we drift to sleep. As your children watch you, what would they say is the greatest love of your life?

LOVING GOD COMPLETELY

Standing upon the cusp of entering the Promised Land, Moses gathered the nation of Israel together for final instructions before embarking upon their long-awaited entry. After forty years of wanderings, the people were finally ready to inherit their land. At this critical juncture, Moses recapped Israel's history and reminded the people concerning God's commands. Before they entered the land, Moses instructed the people of Israel that the most critical task for them was to love God supremely above all else.[1]

> Deuteronomy 6:4 "Hear, O Israel: The LORD our God, the LORD is one. 5 You shall love the LORD your God with all your heart and with all your soul and with all your might. 6 And these words that I command you today shall be on your heart. 7 You shall teach them diligently to your children, and shall talk of them when you sit in your house, and when you walk by the way, and when you lie down, and when you rise. 8 You shall bind them as a sign on your hand, and they shall be as frontlets between your eyes. 9 You shall write them on the doorposts of your house and on your gates.

This passage is referred to as the *shema*, which is a transliteration for the first word in verse six. The word is a command urging the people "to hear" what is about to be stated.[2] More than mere comprehension, Moses desired the people to obey the words they heard. Knowledge of the information without subsequent application would have been pointless.[3] This truth concerning Yahweh's uniqueness was to be the foundation for all other Jewish truths and to communicate the meaning of a monotheistic religion.[4]

When Moses proclaimed, "Hear, O Israel! The LORD is our God, the LORD is one" (Deut 6:4), he was proclaiming the uniqueness of Yahweh compared to other gods. Through the Exodus experience, the Israelites had comprehended the singularity of Yahweh compared to other gods (Exod 15:11).[5] Yahweh's unparalleled nature was to be met with an uncontested devotion of loving God with all their heart, soul, and strength (Deut 6:5).[6] While the book of Deuteronomy is full of commands following this particular command, this plea to love Yahweh serves as the book's thesis with the following material supporting this foundational claim.[7] God's desired response throughout the book of Deuteronomy is that of love (Deut 10:12; 11:1, 13, 22; 13:3; 19:9; 30:6, 16, 20).[8] Obedience is the supreme act of love.[9]

The Israelites did not view the heart to be the residence of the emotions, but rather the heart was understood to be the center of one's thought processes and corresponding will.[10] Therefore, in order to love God, they must decide to love him with their entire hearts due to the preceding love of Yahweh.[11] Yahweh also expected them to love him with all their soul, meaning "the deepest roots" of life.[12] When Moses urged the people to love Yahweh with all of their "strength," he was not referring to their physical capability but more their intense level of desire to love Yahweh.[13] God expected an excessive type of love since that is the type of love with which he first loved the Israelites.[14]

Moses urged parents not to isolate the teaching of Scripture to the public square, but to first teach the truths of Yahweh within their homes to their own children.[15] Followers of Yahweh were supposed to understand Moses' words in this passage

> Moses urged parents not to isolate the teaching of Scripture to the public square, but to teach the truths of Yahweh within their homes to their own children.

so well that they could transmit that information to the following generations. Like an artist chiseling stone, parents were to shape and mold their children spiritually.[16]

While God expected that present generation to obey him, he was also interested in the multigenerational longevity of obedience.[17] According to his instruction, parents who were concerned about their children's spiritual condition would begin to teach them as early as possible in order to develop them spiritually.[18] Moses taught that parents should take every opportunity possible to instruct their children. These foundational truths were so critical to Israel's survival that parents must teach them at every possible moment. God intended for fathers to teach their sons who would teach their sons, and this example of family dedication would ideally never diminish.[19]

The intention of teaching children the ways of the Lord is so that God's rule would infiltrate into every sphere of the Israelites' lives.[20] Moses desired the people to commit the commands to memory in order to integrate them into their lives (Deut. 6:6). As a way of reinforcement, Moses then told the people to adorn their wardrobes and their homes with God's commands. Jews placed frontlets (Deut 6:8) or phylacteries on their foreheads which were small containers holding sacred passages. Jews also took literally Moses' command to write the words on the doorposts (Deut 6:9) in the form of small containers positioned at the doorways filled with scriptural parchments.[21] While many Jews still practice this command literally, God's intention was to see people integrate his words into the entirety of life rather than allowing them to be mere physical adornment.[22]

God's law was intended to permeate every arena of life for the Israelites. Moses' message was to take this teaching and apply it first to the individual, then to the home, and finally within the community.[23] As God called the people entering the Promised Land, he still calls parents to the same task today. Concerned parents will not rely upon religious institutions only to accomplish their biblical responsibility. To ensure the faithfulness of the next generations, parents must teach their children via example to love God with all their heart, with all their mind, and with all their strength.

NEVER TRUST A SKINNY COOK

In the Spring of 2004, I led a mission team from our church to Guatemala. The team was mainly comprised of college students with my pastor and myself leading the endeavor. For Jeff, our senior pastor, that was his first international mission trip. In addition to expanding his heart for the nations, it also served as a very humorous introduction for him to some third-world experiences.

One of those experiences was building our relationship with one particular lady. Rosa, a mother in the village, served as our cook for the entire week we were there. Each night, our team would pile into a bedroom in her home while she cooked us tortillas and black beans. She was a good cook giving out fair portions to each of us except for Jeff. Rosa had a crush on Jeff. Each night, he would get an extra helping of black beans accompanied by a smile. After a few nights, the translator told us that she was interested in Jeff. Rosa's disposition changed from flirtations ways to blatant disgust when Jeff showed her his wedding band. That night, Rosa gave Jeff a disappointed look as she plopped down only one spoonful of black beans.

The rest of the team were given consistent portions all week long. Some of our team members were wary the first night of eating the meal due to the cleanliness of the stove on which it was cooked and the makeup of the room in which we were sitting. I always made a big deal about swallowing graciously whatever was put in front of us on the mission field and that meal was no exception. One college student looked at her plate and said, "Travis, I can't eat this! I think I'm going to throw up just looking at it. How do we even know this is safe to eat?"

"Have you ever heard the expression, 'Never trust a skinny cook?'" I asked this student.

"Yeah. My mom has that phrase on an oven mitt in our kitchen."

"Well, you can trust Rosa."

Truthfully, in an impoverished region, Rosa stood out among her people as a healthy woman who had enough food to eat. While many people looked frail, Rosa was obviously fed well and healthy. While we may have been unaware of how Rosa cooked, we knew that she enjoyed her food and that she was obviously healthy. It was safe to eat and to enjoy. It was obvious that we could trust Rosa.

In our churches. the problem is we have spiritually skinny parents telling children to love God even though they are not following that mandate themselves. Parents command their children to go to church and do what the preachers say, but to apply those messages would be countercultural within their own home. Parents point their children to pastors who say, "Taste and see that the Lord is good" (Ps 34:8), when they have not dined on that course themselves. Our lives show that we are on a different diet.

We cannot teach our children something we have not learned ourselves. Moses commanded parents to love God extremely and then to teach their children to do the same. We cannot force feed a meal for which we have no appetite. The only way to teach the message is by tasting ourselves.

> We cannot teach our children something we have not learned ourselves.

A TRAGIC LEGACY

In order to impact the next generation, parents must not only instruct their children, but we must be mindful of the weight of our example. I will never forget a conversation I had with one of my dear friends in seminary. We had known each other for a while, and I was very close with his family. His father was in ministry and had been a significant mentor in my life as someone who really knew the Word of God. For me, he was the epitome of 2 Timothy 2:15: "Be diligent to present yourself approved to God as a workman who does not need to be ashamed, accurately handling the word of truth." His example made me want to know the truths of the Bible better.

Our conversation was planned because this mentor of mine, my buddy's father, had just experienced a moral implosion. He deserted his wife, isolated himself from his children, and partook of the pleasures of this world at an unhealthy dosage. The shock of the news was so great to me that I felt physically sick upon hearing it.

As we conversed that day, I had to remove any sign that I was personally struggling. I focused on my friend's devastation and tried to put mine to the side. Unsure of exactly what to say, I tried to assure him that God wasn't done with his father (Phil. 1:6). I also warned him of the danger of bitterness. In addition to those pieces of counsel, I also remember telling him, "Let his fall scare you to death. Don't waste this hurt. You never imagined this could happen to your father, but it did, and it could happen to you if you don't stay alert. 1 Corinthians 10:12 says, 'Therefore let him who thinks he stands take heed that he does not fall.'"

What he said next has stuck with me to this day. With tears in his eyes, he looked up at me and with a trembling voice stated, "When I was young, all I wanted was to be a minister like my dad. I hoped that I would have as much success as he did. I wanted to preach all over the place. I wanted to be recognized in the same evangelical circles. Now, after all this, I just want to make it to the end of my life and have my family say that I was a faithful husband and father."

I pray that you, the reader, will not have to experience such a tragedy in your own life before you reorient your pursuits. My friend's father is an example of someone who had the best that church, ministry, and organized religion had to offer. It was an impressive spiritual pedigree. And yet, on the verge of becoming a father himself, that man's son stopped caring about vocational success or associational respect. He wanted to keep his integrity intact and have his children look at him differently from the image he had of his own father at that time.

My friend's father was a very successful minister in our denomination before his fall. Actively taking care of the needs of a church, I'm not sure if he neglected to disciple his own children or not. I do know they comprehended the information contained in God's Word. This father was a vast array of biblical knowledge. Unfortunately, the biggest impact he made on his children was not the information that he taught, but the information he did not apply. Out of all the biblical information he could have taught his son concerning family, the greatest lesson he could have transferred was by staying faithful for the long haul.

Your children are watching you. They know whether your greatest love is television, recreation, work, leisure, or the Kingdom of God. Whether you are riding on the lawnmower, changing channels in the living room, conversing with your spouse, investing your resources, or worshiping in your the church, your children see your example. That lesson will be seared in their minds more than anything else you ever say.

I love being a minister. While I rejoice in my calling and vocation, the hardest element about ministry is when you feel like you are fighting an uphill battle. No matter how stellar our programs or sermons, those momentary calls for a life devoted to loving God are dwarfed when a different message is preached all week in the home. If parents are showing through their lives to love God with part of the heart, a percentage of their soul, and some of their might, it is nearly impossible for another message to break through. More than solely the transfer of biblical information, provide for your children an example of someone whose love for God permeates every part of his or her life. If you want to change your children in order for them to love God, they need to see it first fleshed out through your example.

---

[1] Doug McIntosh and Max E. Anders, Deuteronomy, Holman Old Testament Commentary (Nashville: Broadman and Holman, 2002), 84.

[2] Ibid., 85.

[3] Eugene H. Merrill, Deuteronomy, The New American Commentary, vol. 4 (Nashville: Broadman and Holman, 1994), 162.

[4] James T. Draper, "The Ground of All Truth: Deut. 6:4-9," Faith and Mission 15, no. 2 (1998): 53.

[5] Peter C. Craigie, The Book of Deuteronomy, The New International Commentary on the Old Testament (Grand Rapids: Eerdmans, 1976), 169.

[6] Christopher J. H. Wright, Deuteronomy, New International Biblical Commentary, vol. 4 (Peabody, MA: Hendrickson Publishers, 1996), 98.

[7] Craigie, The Book of Deuteronomy, 169.

[8] Wright, Deuteronomy, 98.

[9] Merrill, Deuteronomy, 163.

[10] McIntosh and Anders, Deuteronomy, 85.

[11] Duane L. Christensen, Deuteronomy, Word Biblical Commentary, vol. 6A (Nashville: Nelson, 2001), 144.

[12] Wright, Deuteronomy, 99.

[13] McIntosh and Anders, Deuteronomy, 86.

[14] Wright, Deuteronomy, 99.

[15] Andreas J. Köstenberger and David W. Jones, God, Marriage & Family: Rebuilding the Biblical Foundation (Wheaton, IL: Crossway, 2004), 107.

[16] Merrill, Deuteronomy, 167.

[17] Ibid., 166.

[18] McIntosh and Anders, Deuteronomy, 86.

[19] Merrill, Deuteronomy, 166-67.

[20] McIntosh and Anders, Deuteronomy, 86.

[21] Craigie, The Book of Deuteronomy, 171.
[22] Wright, Deuteronomy, 100.
[23] Craigie, The Book of Deuteronomy, 171.

CHAPTER 4
AS FOR ME AND MY HOUSE

The name "Tiger Woods" has sparked conversations since he emerged on the PGA Tour. Seen as a young man with great golfing potential. Early in his career, talk became regular concerning his assumed legendary status in the golfing community. Many speculated at one time that he was the most dominant athlete in any sport at any time.

When you look back over his career, Tiger Woods was destined for greatness. When his father began putting golf clubs in his hands at age 3, Tiger never looked back. His father did more than make this a fun photo op, he trained his son to be a legitimate golfer. You can find video footage of Tiger golfing as a young boy on talk shows and news broadcasts. It should come as no surprise that he reached the top of the golfing world at such a young age, for his father instilled that into him with everything that he had.

More recently, his name sparks conversations with a slightly different focus and tone. After the media got wind of a domestic issue involving him and his wife, the world has watched the absolute moral and vocational demise of Tiger Woods. At the time of this writing, not only has his family life been demolished by scandal, but his golfing game has been almost unrecognizable from its former glory. Unless there is some turnaround in the future, history will remember Tiger Woods as one of the best to ever play the game of golf, but his story will always be plagued with unfortunate decisions off the course.

I enjoy playing golf. Well, let me clarify: I enjoy spending time on a golf course attempting to hit the ball. I only started playing golf when I was 27. Not only am I a late starter, I have only golfed about twice a year since. I have come to the realization that I will never catch up with Tiger's golf skills (even in their recent state). No amount of training, lessons, or expensive clubs could ever help me in my lifetime to get to his level. Why? Because his father chose for him a long time ago what the one passion of his life would be.

While Tiger's father has passed away, I often wondered what would have happened if it had not been a golf club placed in Tiger's young hands? Imagine where a child would be spiritually if a father put the Word of God in his child's hands as much as Earl Woods put a putter in the hands of his son. Think about the mistakes Tiger could have avoided. Imagine what his moral values would be. Although his golf game might never have reached the status of his glory days, I wonder if his family would still be intact.

Every father chooses something for his children. They may not come right out and say it, but there is a god in every house. It might be golf, baseball, recognition, promotions, luxury, or a host of other worldly things, but make no mistake - there is a god in every home in America; somebody has to choose which god it will be.

> They may not come right out and say it, but there is a god in every house.

CHOOSING TO SERVE THE LORD

Moses had successfully led God's people out of slavery in Egypt. Due to some disobedience on his behalf, he could not lead Israel into the Promised Land after shepherding these obstinate people in the wilderness for 40 years. Moses died on the border being able to see in the distance the goal for which he had been striving. After Moses' farewell speech, Israel entered the Promised Land with a new leader, Joshua. Following behind the leadership of Moses was no small task, but Joshua rose to the occasion due to God's affirmation (Josh 1:8-9). This military commander led the people to retake the land by force. After years of struggles and wars, they were finally ready to settle in their new land.

Once they had procured the land, Joshua delivers a final word of instruction. In light of all that Israel has experienced, Joshua challenged Israel to determine if they would follow Yahweh exclusively (Josh 24:14-15). At this pivotal moment in their history, Joshua decided to lead the nation no longer as a fearless commander facing Israel's international problems but as a bold preacher combating Israel's spiritual problems. Before he presented the ultimatum, Joshua appealed to God's work in the past among the Israelites.[1] As Joshua relived Israel's history (Josh 24:3-13), he quoted Yahweh's voice and reminded the people that every victorious battle was due to Yahweh's intervention and not the Israelites' strength.

> Joshua 24:14 "Now therefore fear the LORD and serve him in sincerity and in faithfulness. Put away the gods that your fathers served beyond the River and in Egypt, and serve the LORD. 15 And if it is evil in your eyes to serve the LORD, choose this day whom you will serve, whether the gods your fathers served in the region beyond the River, or the gods of the Amorites in whose land you dwell. But as for me and my house, we will serve the LORD."
> 16 Then the people answered, "Far be it from us that we should forsake the LORD to serve other gods, 17 for it is the LORD our God who brought us and our fathers up from the land of Egypt, out of the house of slavery, and who did those great signs in our sight and preserved us in all the way that we went, and among all the peoples through whom we passed. 18 And the LORD drove out before us all the peoples, the Amorites who lived in the land. Therefore we also will serve the LORD, for he is our God."

This passage reflects a covenant in which most often the higher authority would promise something and the vassals would promise something in return. In this covenant, Yahweh appealed to what he has already done, provoking loyalty from the Israelites based on the mere mentioning of his previous involvement in Israel's history.[2] Israel's proper response to this list of divine activity is unwavering allegiance.[3] Joshua did not appeal to Israel's past commitment or accomplishments; instead he reminded the people of their constant idolatry and exhorted them to fear Yahweh.[4]

To fear Yahweh was to possess a deep reverence that led to allegiance and submission.[5] As the Israelites comprehended the massive works of Yahweh and the enormity of his commands, the only proper response was to fear him. In addition to fearing Yahweh, the people were also commanded to serve Yahweh (Josh 24:14). Joshua utilized the word "serve" nine times in this lone section (Josh 24:14-18). He thus informed the Israelites that their level of service to Yahweh was expected to be exemplary.[6]

Joshua urged the people to "throw away the gods your forefathers worshiped beyond the River and in Egypt" (Josh 24:14, 23). Generations removed from Israel's beginning, these people were still bent on following other gods. Regardless of how many times they had seen the superiority of Yahweh compared to other gods, Joshua revealed that these gods were still a permanent presence in the religious life of Israel.

When Joshua referred to the gods "beyond the River," he was referring to the gods Israel had acquired during their travels and the gods of other nations. The gods that the Israelites worshiped in Egypt were the numerous Egyptian gods associated with the land, the sky, the Nile River, and many other elements in Egyptian life.[7] Israel obviously venerated other gods while in

Egypt (Ezek 20:7; 23:3, 8),[8] and Joshua implies that Israel had never been able to purge themselves completely from idol worship.[9] More than just a removal from the heart, Joshua urged the people to remove the idols physically because this act would serve as a public statement concerning their declared devotion.[10]

When Joshua urged the Israelites to "choose this day" whom they would serve (Josh 24:15), he implied an ongoing action rather than simply a onetime decision.[11] Even though this decision had constant implications, he did call on them to make a specific decision for that crucial moment in Israel's history. In this pivotal moment of decision, Joshua did not include any divine threats; he simply asked them to choose.[12] Due to the serious nature of this choice, future generations would be affected.[13] Other nations followed whichever god seemed best suited for each individual crisis, but Israel had a relationship with Yahweh who had proven his mighty capabilities repeatedly.[14] Due to Yahweh's jealousy, he would no longer allow his people to continue to divide their loyalties.[15]

Because Joshua could not decide for the entire nation, he instead declared that he and his household would maintain exclusive commitment to Yahweh.[16] While God was normally the one choosing, he now demanded that the Israelites choose to whom they would be devoted.[17] Once Joshua delivered the ultimatum and proclaimed his family's stance, he then demanded an answer from the people. The people respond positively, but Joshua turned on them and stated that they would be unable to follow Yahweh (Josh 24:19-20). Joshua's unexpected response is "perhaps the most shocking statement in the OT."[18] Yahweh's expected level of commitment was for the Israelites to serve him in every arena of life; due to this standard and Israel's spotted record, Joshua told the people that this task is impossible for them.[19]

The people disagreed with Joshua and promised to commit themselves to Yahweh only (Josh 24:16-18). From their words, it appeared they were genuine in their intention, though history would reveal their unwillingness for follow through.[20] Joshua apparently believed their intention and established a covenant to remind the people of their commitment to Yahweh.[21] This covenant is similar to Near Eastern covenants which reflected the monarchy's protection and provision for the vassals with corresponding allegiance.[22] Joshua commanded the people to serve as their own witnesses, implying they would receive the consequences if they did not fulfill their end of the covenant.[23]

The Book of Judges reveals that the Israelites verbally committed to Yahweh, but they did not keep their promise (Judg 2:11-13; 6:10). Joshua's family proved to be an exception in a country turning from its God.[24] Joshua's example reveals a leader resolved to commitment regardless of what his followers decided.[25] Like Joshua, no follower of God can make a commitment for an entire nation. But in the same passion of Joshua, a father can and should stand up and make that decision for his household.

For so long, Joshua, in his role as Israel's leader, had decided how the nation would respond. Settling into the new normalcy for Israel as they reached the Promised Land, he knew he could not make that decision for the entire nation anymore, but he could make it for his family. No one knows for sure what Joshua's family's spiritual climate was. We don't know if he was dealing with a rebellious teenager or a selfish toddler. No one knows the spiritual devotion of his wife or his children. All we know is that Dad decided that he would choose for his home. Since every home had a god to follow, his would set their hearts to follow Yahweh.

Even if one's culture is choosing to follow every god but Yahweh, the leader of the household must dedicate his or her home to serving the one true God.[26] Joshua's final purpose must have been the establishment of this covenant, as the next scene recorded is Joshua's death (Josh 24:29-30).[27] Joshua's commitment serves as a steadfast example. Children desperately need committed parents who will stand up and decide to follow God no matter what direction the culture is heading. If parents commit their homes to God in speech and in deed, children will reap spiritual benefits.

> Children desperately need committed parents who will stand up and decide to follow God no matter what direction the culture is heading.

PICKING BETWEEN GODS

It was more obvious back in Joshua's day when another god had a family's allegiance due to the shiny statue in the living room. Nowadays, idolatry might not be as blatant but that does not mean it is absent. The lures of this world have many homes within their grasps vying for every ounce of devotion a family can muster. Fathers who teach their sons how to hit a ball more often than they teach them to follow God have made their decisions. Mothers who spend more resources on the outer appearances of their daughters than the internal quality of their hearts have made their decisions. Families who make Jesus an honorable mention in the course of family life rather than the centerpiece of their homes have made their decisions.

    I recently officiated a funeral service for a friend's father. Since this man was not active in any church, they were in desperate need for someone to navigate them through the funeral proceedings. As I conversed with the family, members sincerely believed that this man had professed faith in Christ at one point in his life. As I walked through this family during the grieving process, I asked them to reflect on their father. Each family member shared the same thing concerning this man's life: cars. This man loved cars. He loved to buy them, work on them, display them, and drive them. Standing in the funeral home with the entire family, I discovered this man's legacy was that he liked cars.

    It's hard for me to determine if cars were this man's god or not, but when asked what was the biggest memory of their father, that's all his family could provide. As I drove behind the last car he would ride in as his casket was being transported to the cemetery, I wondered: If I were to die right now, what would my family say was my one thing? If they were to summarize my life's pursuits and communicate the one thing that had my devoted service, what would they say?

    What would your family say about you? That day is coming. One day, your body will be gone and your family and friends will finally talk about you without any concern of repercussion. As they huddle up merely feet away from your casket, what would they say was your one thing? What god did you follow all your days? What thing or person had your heart so tightly that it consumed your thoughts?

You are choosing something now, and your family sees it. It might be a golf club or it might be a Bible, but they all know what it is. Does that mean that golf is evil? No, unless golf steals our hearts so much that it asserts itself into God's rightful place. Whatever it might be, your job is to get rid of those gods you have collected along the way. Remove them from your home. Let there be no question concerning which god to which you belong.

One great step in communicating your desire to your family is to be honest with them about your past mistakes and your future desires. Gather your family together and declare, "As for me and my house, we will serve the Lord. We haven't always put him first. We've brought a lot of things into our home that we have put before him, but today is a new day. We will serve the Lord."

When we were leading our church through a time for families to make Christ the center of the home rather than an honorable mention, I looked for a worship song that a family could sing together to commit themselves to the Lord. Unfortunately, there isn't a lot of material out there. I decided to write a worship song for our church body entitled "Your Home." I prayed that husbands and wives would sing this hand in hand. I prayed that fathers and mothers would sing this over their children. My prayer for them, and for you, is that we would choose to make our homes his home in every room of the house.

YOUR HOME
By Travis Agnew

Verse 1:
We will choose this very day whom we will serve
Give you the praise that you deserve
We will follow our great God, no one else will do
Unite our hearts, we're in desperate need of you

Chorus:
As for me and my house, we will serve the Lord
Led by your Spirit, obeying your Word
Make our home, your home
As for me and my house, in you, we will trust
Love one another the way you love us
Make our home, your home

Verse 2:
God help us humble ourselves and lay down our pride
Help us forgive, your grace as our guide
We will seek your constant help to cherish our vows
Rescue our homes, we're in need of you now

Bridge:
Come renew and restore; take back what is yours
Come and heal our families

---

[1] James Montgomery Boice, Joshua (Grand Rapids: Baker, 2005), 131.

[2] Jerome F. D. Creach, Joshua, Interpretation (Louisville: Westminster John Knox, 2003), 121.

[3] Lai Ling Elizabeth Ngan, "A Teaching Outline for the Book of Joshua," Review and Expositor 95, no. 2 (1998): 167.

[4] Boice, Joshua, 131.

[5] Creach, Joshua, 124.

[6] David M. Howard, Joshua, The New American Commentary, vol. 5 (Nashville: Broadman and Holman, 1998), 435.

[7] Boice, Joshua, 134-35.

[8] Marten H. Woudstra, The Book of Joshua, New International Commentary on the Old Testament (Grand Rapids: Eerdmans, 1981), 351.

[9] Howard, Joshua, 435.

[10] Creach, Joshua, 125.

[11] Boice, Joshua, 134.

[12] Trent C. Butler, Joshua, Word Biblical Commentary, vol. 7 (Waco, TX: Word Books, 1983), 274.

[13] Charles B. Bugg, "Joshua 24:14-18–The Choice," Review and Expositor 95, no. 2 (1998): 279.

[14] Butler, Joshua, 273.

[15] Howard, Joshua, 437.

[16] Richard S. Hess, Joshua: An Introduction and Commentary, The Tyndale Old Testament Commentaries (Leicester, England: InterVarsity Press, 1996), 305.

[17] Howard, Joshua, 436.

[18] Butler, Joshua, 274.

[19] Creach, Joshua, 127.

[20] Howard, Joshua, 438.

[21] Boice, Joshua, 136.

[22] Creach, Joshua, 120-21.

[23] Woudstra, The Book of Joshua, 354.

[24] Hess, Joshua, 305.

[25] Howard, Joshua, 436.

[26] Boice, Joshua, 136.

[27] Creach, Joshua, 120.

CHAPTER 5
GENERATIONAL HAND-ME-DOWNS

I am very lucky I survived my first whitewater rafting trip. Taking a bunch of rowdy teenagers down rapids was a risky endeavor, but our youth minister was up for the challenge. As we jumped off of the buses, we were instructed to divide into groups of six. I was a part of a chauvinistic sextet that wanted to have a guys-only raft so that we could travel exceptionally fast down the rapids. Our patient raft guide attempted to warn us of certain situations to no avail. We were a bunch of "men" who were going to dominate the river.

The first rapid proved to be too much for our manliness. A simple class-two rapid dumped out every guy in our raft as every other raft glided past us gleefully as we scrambled for shore. Upon flipping the raft back over, our raft guide proposed a different plan for the remainder of the trip. "How about we try that I tell you guys what to do, and you do what I tell you? That way, you can stay out of the river and not be the laughingstock of the entire day."

We agreed. For the rest of the day, we listened to that voice in the back of the boat. Playing catchup for the remainder of the trip, we were to eager to paddle right when he said so. We were willing to let the rapids simply take us when needed be, and we were willing to dig in at his command. The rest of the trip proved to be an exciting and yet dry experience.

Our children need a voice in the back of the boat telling them where to go and where not to go. It's especially beneficial if that voice has been down that path before. In the river, we began to trust that voice behind us because he had gone down that river many times before. He knew what worked really well, and he also knew what capsized rafts. Listening to his instructions in the water saved us a lot of pain.

Let's face it: you have lived some life. Your life has contained some moments of brilliance, but I imagine there are also some moments that you wish you could take back. You have walked through trials and temptations, and your scars have stories to tell. The question is: will you be willing to tell your children your stories to ensure they don't have the same scars that you do?

I want you to think back to some of the worst decisions you made growing up. Is there a decision that you regret? Is there a season of life that you wish could be stricken from the memory books? Did you have a period of time in which you are glad Facebook had yet to be invented so there wasn't mobile phone uploads of your behavior?

You made mistakes. You have regrets. Do you honestly want your children to repeat some of your wayward ways? Of course not. You pray that your children will not indulge in some of those things that had your attention once. What if I told you that you could shortcut them in life? They could avoid some of those traps if only someone would be in the back of the boat warning them of oncoming danger.

> Do you honestly want your children to repeat some of your wayward ways?

WARN THE NEXT GENERATION

In Psalm 78, the psalmist retells periods of Israel's sinful past in hope that the present generation can avoid future transgressions.[1] This historical psalm recounting Israel's sinful past is the second longest psalm, exceeded only by the lengthy Psalm 119.[2] By the psalm's form, a priest probably addressed the nation of Israel as his people (Ps 78:1) and delivered the message recorded in Psalm 78.[3]

> Psalm 78:1
> Give ear, O my people, to my teaching;
> > incline your ears to the words of my mouth!
> > 2 I will open my mouth in a parable;
> > I will utter dark sayings from of old,
> 3 things that we have heard and known,
> > that our fathers have told us.
> 4 We will not hide them from their children,

> but tell to the coming generation
> the glorious deeds of the LORD, and his might,
> and the wonders that he has done
>
> 5 He established a testimony in Jacob
> and appointed a law in Israel,
> which he commanded our fathers
> to teach to their children,
> 6 that the next generation might know them,
> the children yet unborn,
> and arise and tell them to their children,
> 7 so that they should set their hope in God
> and not forget the works of God,
> but keep his commandments;
> 8 and that they should not be like their fathers,
> a stubborn and rebellious generation,
> a generation whose heart was not steadfast,
> whose spirit was not faithful to God.

Before the psalmist recounts objective details of how Israel transgressed against the Lord throughout history, he sought first to illuminate the Israelites concerning the actual spiritual significance (Ps 78:1-3).[4] The psalmist commanded the hearers to pay attention to these critical words. Since certain elements are absent from this history, the psalmist had purpose in including certain information and neglecting other information.[5] By the psalmist's providing certain information, the hearer should be able to make certain conclusions.[6]

While Israel might have desired to forget the past mistakes, those stories are remembered to warn of future possible apostasy (Ps 78:4-7).[7] As the psalmist relayed their history, a faithful God is pitted against a faithless people. The psalmist hailed Yahweh for his redemptive deeds in Israel's history. In this psalm, the psalmist appealed to four different generations: the hearers, the ancestors, the future descendants, and the next generation.[8] The psalmist desired that "from generation to generation, God's ways and will are to be passed on for children to learn from the sins of their fathers and for God to be known as mighty and glorious."[9] If parents are to offer their children any type of education, they must educate their children concerning Yahweh's deeds.

If the psalmist's opening message were not clear enough, he then exhorted his hearers simply not to be like their forefathers (Ps 78:8). The present generation was to remember both the great deeds of Yahweh and the disappointing deeds of their forefathers in order to stay faithful to Yahweh.[10] He established a testimony for himself through the people of Israel (Ps 78:5) in order that they serve as a beacon of truth in a world full of idolatrous people.[11] In this psalm, the psalmist attempted to educate Israel concerning Yahweh's past miracles, his commandments to the people, and his reminders of the Law.[12]

If the psalmist were successful in transmitting this information, he also hoped that generation would be faithful to transmit that same message to the next generation (Ps 78:6). Each new generation has an advantage over the last generation in that they can see another example of the consequences of unfaithful living. If this generation were wise, it would turn away from imitating their forefathers' examples.[13]

Parents of every generation can learn a great lesson from this psalm: children do not have to make the same mistakes as their parents. Whether referring to personal unholiness or national idolatry, parents can educate their children of trodden sinful paths in order to persuade the next generation to follow a different course. In addition to warning children about past apostasy, parents should also inform their children concerning the past wondrous deeds of the Lord. Children of Christian parents might be amazed to hear the testimonies of their parents concerning how God worked in their lives. If parents would apply this psalmist's words today, many children would possess a greater foundation needed to forsake sinful choices and embrace a powerful, proven God.

THE FAMILY HISTORY

Studying this passage made me think about the lessons that were available to me through my family history. Many lessons had already been received at the school of hard knocks, and I would rather read the cliff notes than get a front row seat of similar mistakes being made in my life. So when I decided to interview my parents casually, I kept asking myself: "Are you sure you really want to go down this road?" At that time, more and more marriages around me were falling apart, and pastors' marriages were no exclusion. I earnestly desired to glean wisdom from anyone who was willing to be transparent with me. Since I can't ask for parents who love me and my family more than what mine do, I wanted to learn from them. I needed to know what they did well. I wanted to know what they would change if they could.

Over the series of many different conversations with each of them, I simply sought their wisdom and experiences. I reassured them that nothing that they could say could make me love them any less. I was not anticipating disappointing conversations. I was asking my mom and my dad, who both love me like crazy, to help me avoid any possible pitfalls along the way. In these conversations, we would talk about marriage, parenting, and faith. We spoke of the different trials and temptations that are present in different stages of life. With both my mom and my dad, I received some very enlightening information. In many ways, I was finally able to put all the pieces together concerning our family history and dynamics.

As a result of those conversations, I learned many invaluable lessons. First, my parents had a lot of wisdom that I had not received because I simply failed to ask. Second, I realized that every temptation is common to man (1 Cor 10:13). Finally, I had greater respect for my parents than ever before. A common fear about delving into the past is that images might be tarnished and things never be the same again. Hearing their triumphs and tragedies provided an invaluable guide for me as I navigated my way in the early stages of marriage and parenthood.

THE POWER OF YOUR STORY

One of your children's most beloved books in your home might soon be your high school yearbook.

Your children know you as a responsible (or somewhat responsible) adult fully equipped with bills, a job, and a minivan, yet before they ever knew you, a lot of your life had already been lived. Seeing your extracurricular activities, fashion statements, and funny hairdos in your yearbook open up an entire new world to them concerning your life.

Most parents became followers of Christ before their children were around. Even if you became a Christian later in life, your personal testimony is not information that they inherently receive. The greatest story you will ever tell your children will be God's story of how he brought redemption to mankind. The 2nd greatest story will be how your story intersected with God's story – the story of your salvation.

As your children grow, they will have different levels of doubt concerning the Christian faith. You might even experience a child arguing with you concerning your personal beliefs. While they may resort to arguments, they can't argue with results. One of the greatest ways to teach your children concerning salvation and walking with Christ is by sharing your personal testimony with them.

If you have truly been changed by the gospel, they can't argue with the fact that Jesus changed you. Depending upon the age, you will use different wording or select different portions of your story to tell, but you can't begin too early sharing with your children how Christ made all things new in your life.

The psalmist showed the need for parents to speak to their children concerning three things: 1) the faithfulness of God, 2) the frailties of that generation, and

3) the potential of the next generation. He teaches parents that if they can only share their personal shortcomings, possibly their children could bypass some of those mistakes. By no means do I recommend sharing all the gory details of your past. Details are not needed. You want to equip your children with lessons to protect them from mistakes, not scar them for life with war stories of your own. Share with your children the big picture of how life can get off track if you don't keep God first.

While it is ideal for parents to teach their children the goodness of God and frailty of mankind earlier in a child's life rather than later, unfortunately, that is not what usually happens. Realistically, many parents are faced with a crisis in a child's life that brings about guilt and regret. In those moments, many parents wish they would have been more forthright with their children than what they were.

As a minister, I normally have plenty of words to share in a counseling session, but one particular meeting with some parents left me near speechless. This couple had come to see me for guidance in dealing with their collegiate daughter. Enjoying to the hilt all that college could provide, her appetite never seemed fully quenched. She was bouncing from guy to guy, dropping classes like it was her hobby, and partying at a dangerous level.

These concerned parents came to me to see what I could do to make their daughter change her life. Her latest escapade had collected quite the array of consequences to accompany her behavior, and they were seeking assistance to get her back on the right track. Mortified by her choices, these parents were bewildered by how she got herself into this situation. The pacifist in me wanted to encourage them and lead them in prayer. The Spirit of God in me had another idea. I was beckoned to speak the truth in love to this couple (Eph 4:15).

Why were we shocked that this young lady had gotten pregnant out of wedlock when that is exactly what her parents had done? Why was everyone scratching their heads as to why this girl would succumb to temptation after temptation when her parents had lived that same lifestyle before they straightened up? Everyone was wondering how such a "nice, Christian girl" could get in such a dilemma, and yet her parents never warned her concerning the dead end of that already trodden path.

Parents want the best for their children. Would you be willing to give the best to your children if it included getting intentional and personal? Once again, your children do not need to hear every sordid detail, but hearing the stories of your positive and negative choices could spare them from repeating the same mistakes and living through some of the same consequences you had to endure.

Sometimes teaching your kids to follow God means that you must tell them that they shouldn't follow your example. The greatest admission to your children might be that you have not been perfect but how we are all in need of God's grace daily. Provide that voice in the back of the raft showing the next generation the way. As you share

> Sometimes teaching your kids to follow God means that you must tell them that they shouldn't follow your example.

with them the mistakes you have made, do not neglect to remind them concerning the faithfulness and grace of our God which has kept you to this day and can keep them as well.

---

[1] Steven J. Lawson and Max E. Anders, Psalms 76-150, Holman Old Testament Commentary, vol. 12 (Nashville: Broadman and Holman, 2006), 14.

[2] Richard J. Clifford, Psalms 73-150, Abingdon Old Testament Commentaries (Nashville: Abingdon, 2003), 43.

[3] Hans-Joachim Kraus, Psalms 60-150: A Commentary (Minneapolis: Augsburg, 1989), 123.

[4] Lawson and Anders, Psalms 76-150, 14.

[5] Marvin E. Tate, Psalms 51-100, Word Biblical Commentary, vol. 20 (Dallas: Word, 1990), 284.

[6] Derek Kidner, Psalms 73-150, The Tyndale Old Testament Commentaries (Leicester, England: InterVarsity, 1973), 281.

[7] Lawson and Anders, Psalms 76-150, 14.

[8] John M. Drescher, Parents: Passing the Torch of Faith (Scottdale, PA: Herald Press, 1997), 27.

[9] Köstenberger and Jones, God, Marriage & Family, 102.

[10] Kraus, Psalms 60-150, 126.

[11] Charles Spurgeon and Roy Clarke, The Treasury of David (Nashville: Nelson, 1997), 673.

[12] Drescher, Parents, 27.

[13] Spurgeon and Clarke, The Treasury of David, 673-74.

CHAPTER 6
THE IMPORTANCE OF FATHERS

My wife and I arrived early for the Focus on Marriage simulcast held at our church. On February 27, 2010, churches from all over the United States linked up to focus on the sacredness of marriage vows. Realizing that everything for the simulcast was working properly, I found a seat and began flipping through the workbook.

We were a couple of months away from our second child, Eli, arriving, and so we were thankful to have this day to focus on marriage ourselves. I had just graduated with my doctorate in December which had consumed a lot of extra time in the previous thirty months. Most of those nights when my wife would go to bed, I would crawl back to my computer to work on much of the material addressed in this book. After all that focused time on parenting, one advertisement in the workbook leaped off the page to me.

"From the makers of *Fireproof* - coming 2011 - *Courageous*." The remainder of the page highlighted the upcoming movie that would be released by Sherwood Pictures which would focus on fathers. Since so much of my research showed the pivotal role of fathers in that process, I almost jumped to my feet in excitement. *Fireproof* had made such an impact on our marriage and countless others, I was so thrilled that the same attention was going to be focused upon fathers. In my seat, waiting for the simulcast to begin, I began to pray for *Courageous*.

"God, use this movie in a mighty way. Make it quality, but not for quality's sake. Make it quality to reach homes in our community. Change the nation through this movement. Bring the hearts of the fathers back to their children. Raise men up in this country to be the primary evangelists and disciple-makers of their children. Lord, raise up people to help this movie impact homes, churches, and communities. Please God, prepare the workers of those that will be involved in making the movie, but also those who will help develop the next steps from the movies so your churches can disciple fathers all over. Lord, please change the fathers in this country."

You might think that I am making the next part of this story up, and I would understand because I was quite shocked too. A few moments after I said "amen," my phone vibrated in my pocket indicating a new email had been received. When I pulled up the application, the subject line said, "Courageous." Needless to say, I was intrigued to what this email was about.

The email was sent from an editor at LifeWay Christian Resources. She assumed that I wasn't aware of the upcoming movie entitled, *Courageous*, but she wanted to know if I would be interested in developing a Bible study curriculum to accompany the movie's release dealing with the biblical standard of fatherhood. She explained what appeared to be a random string of events that put me on the radar for this project, but as I read further, I was overwhelmed at how God had brought all of this together. I wasn't aware that moments before I had been praying for myself!

Over the next year, I was blessed to be able to work with LifeWay and Sherwood Pictures to develop a curriculum entitled, "Honor Begins at Home." I remember one particular conversation with Stephen Kendrick while working in Nashville where he warned me concerning the spiritual warfare that would come my family's way if I signed up to partner with them. Obviously, God wanted to use this project, and it was also apparent that the enemy was desiring to stop any attempt to raise the bar for Christian fathers. The next few months would prove Stephen's words to be true as my family faced one trying circumstance after another. With each obstacle, I was tempted not to be the father that God had called me to be. It almost felt as when I, as a father, pushed through the circumstances, God was validating my work in an attempt to raise the bar for other fathers.

Battling through constant warfare, my time in God's Word sustained me. Out of all the passages I studied, Ephesians 6 threw one of the biggest curve balls concerning parenthood. While the passage speaks to the role of both father and mother, the Apostle Paul singles out fathers in a surprising way.

SINGLED OUT

> Ephesians 6:1 Children, obey your parents in the Lord, for this is right. 2 "Honor your father and mother" (this is the first commandment with a promise), 3 "that it may go well with you and that you may live long in the land." 4 Fathers, do not provoke your children to anger, but bring them up in the discipline and instruction of the Lord.

As Paul neared the conclusion of his letter to the Ephesians, he included instructions concerning the family. His first instructions in chapter six were for children to obey their parents (Eph 6:1). The phrase "in the Lord" is not to be understood as obeying Christian parents only, but children were expected to obey their parents regardless of the parents' spiritual standing.[1] For children without ideal Christian parents, honor for the individual parent may be difficult at times, but Christian children must muster honor for at least the office of parent at all times.[2]

Paul's command to obey parents in the Lord adds a deeper spiritual implication to the command. Children must understand that when they obey their parents, they are also obeying the Lord.[3] Paul viewed this obedience so significantly that he grouped disobedience to parents in a list of sins next to murder, greed, and other unrighteous acts (Rom 1:28-32). One of Paul's signs that the end of time is nearing is the presence of disobedient children (2 Tim 3:2).

Paul provided no indication that problems existed in the Ephesian church concerning family relationships, but he obviously saw the need to regard family instruction as an appropriate teaching regardless of circumstances.[4] For many Christians, the home is often the most difficult environment to live with the attitude of Christ (Phil 2:3-5), but Paul held this environment to be one of the most critical in which to show mutual honor.[5] Not only did Paul instruct children to obey their parents in the Lord, but he also told this church that obedience is simply the just act for children according to God's plan for the family.[6]

While the term translated "children" could refer to adult children, Paul probably intended his message for younger children who were still impressionable and prime for spiritual molding.[7] Paul might have intended his message for teenagers who were not old enough to live on their own but still young enough to receive discipline.[8] Even though this commandment is meant more toward younger children, honoring parents is a commandment to be kept in some sense throughout a lifetime. As young children grow into adults, the specifics of obedience will change, but the parents' divine right of honor should never change.[9]

While the command for children to obey their parents originated at the giving of the Ten Commandments (Exod 20:12), the New Testament includes this command five times other than this passage (Matt 15:4; 19:19; Mark 7:10; 10:19; Luke 18:20).[10] God's original command (Exod 20:12; Deut 5:16) instructed children to obey in order to flourish in the land. Paul, speaking to Jews and Gentiles removed from the idea of inheriting land that the original hearers anticipated, changed the ending from "live long in the land" to "live long on the earth" (Eph 6:3). This subtle shift indicates that his audience was not anticipating prospering in a certain geographical location, but they did desire for their lives to prosper in general.[11] Paul's intention through this subtle change was to indicate that obedience to parents provides needed structure in the lives of children.[12]

At this point in the passage, the Apostle Paul writes something a little unexpected. After Paul instructed the manner in which children should obey their parents, he then turned his focus to the role of fathers specifically concerning discipline and instruction (Eph 6:4). Paul's distinction between obedience and instruction must be noted. He instructed children to obey both their fathers and mothers, but he exhorted solely fathers to instruct their children.[13] While both parents should be involved in a child's spiritual education, Paul placed the ultimate responsibility upon the fathers (Eph 6:4).[14]

> While both parents should be involved in a child's spiritual education, Paul placed the ultimate responsibility upon the fathers.

Throughout Scripture, God expected fathers to train their children in the way of the Lord. God's disgust with Eli the priest was due to his indifferent attitude toward his godless sons (1 Sam 3:13). In God's plan, a father is responsible for instructing a child, but a child is responsible to obey both a father and a mother.[15]

While fathers are singled out in this passage, Paul looks out for both sons and daughters. Paul's use of the term "children" instead of "sons" (Eph 6:4) is also significant since traditionally girls were not educated like the boys. Although girls were not allowed the same type of societal education as boys, Paul implied that they deserved the same type of spiritual education.[16]

God intends for fathers to discipline their children (Prov 13:24), for God himself as a father disciplines his children as indication of his love (Heb 12:6; Prov 3:12; Ps 119:75; Rev 3:19). While discipline is necessary, God intends parental discipline to bring about Christlike character and not angered resentment (Eph 6:4). If fathers discipline too severely, children could respond with rebellion rather than desired obedience.[17] More often than not, "hostile homes produce hostile children."[18] Paul urged fathers not to become angry themselves, which reiterated his previous instructions concerning anger (Eph 4:26, 27, 31).[19]

In Paul's society, the father had no real restriction upon how he should manage his household. While mothers were granted no legal rights at that time, fathers actually had the legal right to drown their weak or disfigured children and even maintained rights over their grandchildren if they were not living in the same home.[20] Fathers were also permitted to punish as harshly as they deemed necessary, and fatherhood of the day unfortunately avoided pampering, playing, or laughing with one's children.[21] In contrast to the common practice of the time, Paul urged fathers not to discipline too severely or irrationally.

Scripturally, parents are to view children as a gift from God (Ps 127:3).[22] Christian fathers should never merely endure their children, but they are to nurture their children joyfully.[23] Paul desired that healthy fatherly relationship would help stimulate healthy relationships with their father God. Many children will turn away from the Lord, but it is unfortunate when the harshness or the hypocrisy of a child's father is one cause of their rebellion.

Paul expected fathers to discipline themselves before they discipline their children.[24] When fathers raise their children in the instruction of the Lord (Eph 6:4), children should develop Christlike characteristics. A father's rational and compassionate discipline should produce a gentle child (2 Cor 10:1).[25] This godly type of instruction is also reminiscent of Paul's earlier teaching on Christian instruction (Eph 4:20-21).[26] During this time, children were beginning to go to school for formal education, but fathers were still viewed as the primary teacher.

In homes where children are not growing spiritually, one will often unfortunately discover apathetic parents not living up to their God-given responsibilities.[27] Paul desired this church to instruct one another in Christian teaching, but he never saw that task as isolated to the religious institutions.[28] Parents were expected to do their job. Paul's instruction is reminiscent of the words in the book of Proverbs which state, "Train up a child in the way he should go, and when he is old he will not depart from it" (Prov 22:6).[29] God expects fathers not only to discipline their children, but they are also to disciple their children. Fathers are to discipline their children according to God's standards and disciple their children using God's commandments. For successful biblical parenting to take place within the home, parents must live according to their God-given authority coupled with their God-given responsibility.[30]

DADDY'S ARMS IN THE MIDDLE OF A TORNADO

One night, my wife woke me at 5:20 by yelling, "Tornado! Trav, get Obadiah!" In a daze, I ran through the house to a sound that seemed like the windows were about to shatter and the house was about to be lifted above the foundation. Obadiah was still asleep as I scooped him up into my arms. He was startled by the sudden intrusion, and then he seemed to be even more alarmed by the sounds he was hearing. As the sounds escalated, he seemed to be aware that the situation was definitely uncommon.

I was trying to hold him down to protect him and hoping he would stay asleep. He popped his head up as I was carrying him. He looked through the window at the rain coming down and the wind blowing everything in its path. He then looked at me, smiled, pointed at my face, said "Dada" in the most tender voice I have ever heard, and then he laid his head down on my shoulder and went back to sleep.

You must understand this: at this age, if you woke Obadiah up, he stayed up. He usually would not go back down easily. He normally would think it would be time to play. Given the sounds in our home, he should have been alarmed, but instead he fell back asleep. I was eventually able to put him back in his crib once the storm passed. Something was different that night. As he looked at his father in the midst of the storm, he felt peaceful enough to fall back asleep.

For children, a supernatural security should be found in the arms of their fathers. When torrential storms appear or unstable circumstances arise, children should be able to look to their fathers for comfort and safety. Unfortunately, fathers are often known more for their inconsistency than their reliability and resolve.

> Unfortunately, fathers are often known more for their inconsistency than their reliability and resolve.

One Sunday morning, I led a prayer time during worship that wrecked me for days. We had a time when people could come down to the altar in our services and fill out a card that said, "God, if only You could..." and they were to fill in the prayer request. After they took those requests to God, they left those cards on the altar.

The following week, our staff started going through the huge stack of prayer requests. When I got the stack from the stage, the card on top floored me. The handwriting gave it away that this card belonged to a child. Written in pencil, some child in our congregation prayed these words: "*God, if only You could change Daddy's wase. And mack him a better person. and becom a better cerichen.*"

I still pray for this unknown child quite often. I also pray for the child's father. While my heart breaks for this family, it also causes me to reflect what my children would pray for me. Would they pray that Daddy would change his ways? Have I provoked them to anger?

Would they pray that I become a better Christian? Have they seen and heard Jesus through me?

Fathers, God singled you out for a reason. This pinpointing of fathers does not mean that mothers do not have a pivotal role, it just means that God has made our hearts to need a consistent father. I believe God singled out fathers in this passage because he knew that most mothers would normally do their job. Men, it's time to step up and lead your home. God provided no acceptable substitute.

---

[1] Klyne Snodgrass, Ephesians: from Biblical Text...to Contemporary Life, The NIV Application Commentary (Grand Rapids: Zondervan, 1996), 321.

[2] Ibid., 326.

[3] Andrew T. Lincoln, Ephesians, Word Biblical Commentary, vol. 42 (Dallas: Word, 1990), 396.

[4] Ibid., 397.

[5] Snodgrass, Ephesians, 329.

[6] Lincoln, Ephesians, 403.

[7] Snodgrass, Ephesians, 321.

[8] Lincoln, Ephesians, 403.

[9] Snodgrass, Ephesians, 326.

[10] F. F. Bruce, The Epistles to the Colossians, to Philemon, and to the Ephesians, The New International Commentary on the New Testament (Grand Rapids: Eerdmans, 1984), 321.

[11] Ibid., 398.

[12] Snodgrass, Ephesians, 322.

[13] Köstenberger and Jones, God, Marriage & Family, 123.

[14] Lincoln, Ephesians, 400.

[15] Ibid., 406-07.

[16] Snodgrass, Ephesians, 322.

[17] Bruce, The Epistles to the Colossians, to Philemon, and to the Ephesians, 398.

[18] Snodgrass, Ephesians, 325.

[19] Lincoln, Ephesians, 397.

[20] Ibid., 399.

[21] Snodgrass, Ephesians, 325.

[22] Lincoln, Ephesians, 400.

[23] Snodgrass, Ephesians, 326.

[24] Ibid., 329-30.

[25] Bruce, The Epistles to the Colossians, to Philemon, and to the Ephesians, 398.

[26] Lincoln, Ephesians, 397.

[27] Ibid., 400.

[28] Ibid., 408.

[29] Ibid., 400.

[30] Ibid., 409.

CHAPTER 7
A LESS-THAN-IDEAL HOME

In the months leading up to the opening weekend of *Courageous*, I was asked to speak at various churches or functions concerning my role with the film. While I had access to the script and an early edit of the film, I was bound by certain stipulations concerning what I could or could not say about the film. Since I was only a part of the curriculum development process, I would share my story of how I got connected with the film, but then I normally would preach from Ephesians 6 and explain the pivotal nature of fathers in the lives of children.

The same thing happened in every church at which I spoke. While I taught on the irreplaceable role of fathers, I could identify the single mothers in the congregation by their desperate attempts to keep their emotions at bay. In those moments, I was tempted to soften my appeal to fathers.

In every church, I spent time with a weepy mother as she tried to receive counseling from me — while also trying to make sure her kids didn't burn the church down as they impatiently waited for their mom to finish conversing with the preacher. I heard different stories with similar threads. Each of the stories ended with an absentee father and a mother trying to give her children the best that she could provide on her own.

In those moments, I was tempted to back down on my previous claims presented in my sermon. While my heart was breaking for these single moms, I couldn't back down from the biblical truth or the simple reality: children need godly fathers. The scenario of a godly father leading the home is unashamedly God's ideal. The problem is that the ideal is now a diminishing reality for a large percentage of homes.

Unfortunately, I cannot back down in stating that the ideal situation is for the father to lead the charge. Understanding this to be the ideal, I must also share another piece of information with you: God is still the Father to the fatherless (Ps 68:5), and he specializes in bringing beauty from the ashes (Is 61:3). What your child may lack in an earthly father is overshadowed by all that he or she has in a Heavenly Father. As mentioned earlier, none of the biblical families would be labeled as ideal; yet God used people with unfortunate pasts to change the future. Even Jesus' earthly family line was filled with troubled characters.

> What your child may lack in an earthly father is overshadowed by all that he or she has in a Heavenly Father.

In 2 Timothy 1, Paul provides insight into the family of Timothy. Paul's "son-in-the-faith," Timothy, was an early church pastor trusted by Paul. This pastor came from a less-than-ideal home, and God used the women in his family and a step-in father figure to make him into a pastor who would change his community.

THE FAMILY FAITH

2 Timothy 1:3 I thank God whom I serve, as did my ancestors, with a clear conscience, as I remember you constantly in my prayers night and day. 4 As I remember your tears, I long to see you, that I may be filled with joy. 5 I am reminded of your sincere faith, a faith that dwelt first in your grandmother Lois and your mother Eunice and now, I am sure, dwells in you as well. 6 For this reason I remind you to fan into flame the gift of God, which is in you through the laying on of my hands, 7 for God gave us a spirit not of fear but of power and love and self-control.

In Paul's introductory comments of his second letter to Timothy, the apostle indicated that his prayers for his son-in-the-faith had been constant.[1] In the tumultuous times surrounding his ministry, Paul revealed his consistent prayer life toward his mentees.[2] Paul observed a genuine faith in Timothy (2 Tim 1:5), and he prayed that Timothy would be a faithful minister of the gospel.[3]

As Paul described his own faith and the involvement of his family in his own spiritual upbringing (2

Tim 1:1-3), he then wrote of how Timothy's journey is similar to his (2 Tim 1:4-5).[4] While Paul regularly confronted Jews concerning the need for Christ, in this passage, he showed gratitude for his and Timothy's Jewish spiritual heritage,[5] a heritage that Paul often esteems due to his impressive Jewish education (Rom 7:12; Phil 3:4-6).[6]

Paul's first impression of Timothy was a young man possessing genuine Jewish faith due to the involvement of his mother and his grandmother.[7] These women showed evidence of being God-fearing Jews since they were able to recognize the Jewish Messiah in the person of Jesus (Rom 2:28-29).[8] Timothy's mother is first referenced in Acts 16, but this passage is the only record of her name, Eunice. Lois, his grandmother, is mentioned only in this passage.[9]

Luke records Paul's first interaction with Timothy and his family (Acts 16:1-3). Timothy's mother, Eunice, was Jewish, but his father was a Gentile. Jewish circles viewed Timothy negatively concerning his Jewishness since he was not circumcised, but Gentiles essentially viewed him as a Jew.[10] Lois is believed to be Eunice's mother since both are believers, and Timothy's father is never referenced as a believer.[11]

Timothy's father is assumed not to possess saving faith, considering that Luke referenced his unwillingness to circumcise his son (Acts 16:1, 3). Whereas he is never mentioned again, most believe that he was never involved in the church. Some scholars believe that Timothy's father was dead at the time of Timothy's first encounter with Paul, as the verb states that Timothy's father "was a Greek" in the past tense.[12] In the absence of

Timothy's father, Paul served Timothy in a fatherly role.[13] Foreseeing the problems that Timothy would face as a minister in a religion comprised of many converted Jews, Paul had Timothy circumcised to quiet possible opponents.[14]

In his letter, Paul exhorted Timothy to persevere in order to endure the obstacles of ministry. As Paul attempted to instill perseverance in Timothy, he reminded Timothy of the perseverance that his mother Eunice and his grandmother Lois possessed.[15] In the struggles of ministry, Paul encouraged Timothy to endure for the sake of his family's legacy.[16] Paul urged Timothy to recall his privileged familial spirituality and never to retreat from that commitment to God.[17]

Surprisingly, this epistle addressed to Timothy does not begin with ministry strategies or pastoral advice, but rather with praise concerning multigenerational faithfulness. Within a short amount of time since the church's inception, Paul was revealing the impact that family members can have on their relatives' spiritual health.[18]

Every person possesses spiritual ancestry, whether it is positive or negative. While each individual must come to Christ on his or her own regardless of one's family's spirituality, people can begin at an advantage when family members display and share a genuine faith.[19] Eunice and Lois were faithful Jews who taught Timothy the Jewish sacred writings (2 Tim 3:15),[20] but once they converted to Christianity, this change had a significant impact on Timothy's life.[21]

While Timothy was at a spiritual disadvantage — not having a believing father in the home — Timothy's example serves as encouragement to people in similar homes. The absence of Timothy's father was compensated for by his mother, his grandmother, and a volunteer father figure.[22] Considering the absence of Timothy's father, Paul served the role of a spiritual father who served as a role model and encouraged him in the ministry.[23] Even if a home is less-than-ideal, God is able to use whatever resources available to impact a child spiritually. The people used to impact Timothy reveal an effective partnership between a family and a local church.

Only God knows the impact that Timothy had on the Church at Ephesus. Without the influence of Timothy's mother and grandmother, this church could have missed out from his leadership.[24] Many families are not in the ideal situation, much like Timothy's family was not. Timothy's example proves that no matter what the family situation is, lives transformed by Christ can counterbalance any disadvantage. No matter what role a family member possesses, that person can positively impact a relative for Christ and change future generations and even congregations due to his or her faithfulness.[25]

SINGLE-PARENT HOMES

Divorce is plaguing the Church. Statistics are essentially the same concerning the divorce rates for Christians and non-Christians. Fatherlessness is like a cancer sweeping through our country. While both men and women leave their families to follow other pursuits, more often, men are leaving behind single moms to work overtime within the home.

In some homes, two spouses physically live in the same house, but one parent practically exists as a single parent. Married to a detached, inconsistent spouse, one parent often carries the spiritual and emotional weight of raising children. Whether you are legally or practically separated from your spouse, the challenges are great in either situation.

The way in which you handle yourself in front of your children will speak volumes to them. Believe that God is able to do extraordinary things through broken situations. Timothy's mother, Eunice, is remembered for her faith in God, not her complaints concerning her unbelieving husband. If your spouse is out of the picture, make sure to focus on the hope found in all that Jesus provides and not on all the heartache that your ex has brought.

If your ex-spouse is remarried, be cautious how you speak of your children's stepparent. No matter who is mostly to blame for your divorce, as a believer, you are still called to live at peace with everyone as much as it depends on you (Rom 12:18). Refrain from teaching your children bitterness, and show them Christ in the way that you forgive all the people who are involved in your child's life.

One other word of caution: in your desire to provide a stable family for your children, don't settle for anything less than God's best concerning a new spouse. Oftentimes, a lonely and desperate parent will date or marry someone to fill an empty seat at the dinner table. There is some thing worse than being single: getting remarried to someone who does not love God and can do more damage to you and to your children over time.

For those who have lost a spouse in death, the same applies to you. Be wise in how you go forward. Your children do not need a simple replacement. Trust God that in your attempts to follow him, God will do exceedingly abundantly of what you ask of him (Eph 3:20) as you raise your children.

A GRANDMOTHER'S LEGACY

Lois was seen as a pillar in Timothy's life. If you are a grandparent, let this inspire you to a calling in this new phase of life. While it is a favorite pastime of grandparents to spoil their grandchildren, make it all-the-more important to display your personal faith in the Lord before the next generations. Don't advertise your faith as mere church attendance; make it personal in the way you live your life.

> Don't advertise your faith as mere church attendance; make it personal in the way you live your life.

If you are an empty-nester, your opportunity to impact your children or your grandchildren still exists. Many parents in our church were consumed with regret once we began revealing God's plan for parent-driven discipleship. Instead of living in guilt, many of these parents began having conversations with their adult children that they should have had a long time ago. Many of those conversations began by saying, "You know, son, I have recently realized that I didn't do all that God wanted me to do when you were still in the home. I took you to church, but I rarely talked to you about my personal walk with Christ. Do you mind if I share with you some of the things that God has been teaching me lately?"

Talk about an impact! A humble, transparent parent having a spiritual conversation with his or her adult child will leave a lasting impact. Many in our church took a stand like Lois and changed the lives of their own Eunice and Timothy. As a grandparent, God still has a purpose for you in this generation to make an impact for his Kingdom (Acts 13:36).

STEPPING UP

I would be remiss if I did not include in this chapter an appeal for men and women to step into the lives of some children who are less fortunate. As Paul served as a father figure in Timothy's life where there was an unfortunate void, your church, your community, and this world are filled with children who are without parents. Some of those children live in homes where they are not valued or taught, and some of those children are placed in an orphanage or group homes.

If I began to write concerning the need for Christians to step in an nurture orphans and neglected children in this world, this book would get considerably longer. In short, I beg you to pray concerning what your role may be to step into the lives of those who are in a less-than-ideal situation. As you care for the children in your home, please be mindful of those across the street and around the world who need you as well.

Maybe God is calling your family to adopt a child into your home just like he called our family. Or maybe you could serve as foster parents. You could assist foster parents by getting involved in respite care and providing temporary childcare for those foster children when that family was in need. You may just know some teenagers in the church who could join your family on a camping trip, or a young boy who could use a soccer coach. Whatever the need is, you will never regret being the hands and feet of God to provide love and consistency for children who are loved by God.

When God called us to adopt, we had one child in the home who was only one year-old. We felt compassion for the orphans of the world, but we always expected we would put "feet" to our compassion later in life. As God showed us, we had an extra bed in our home that was not being used at the time. God led us in a journey of adoption that changed us forever. God has given us children through different manners, but each of them are unmistakably our children, and we couldn't imagine our home without each child God has placed there.

You might be concerned that caring for other children will take attention away from your own. As long as you continue to provide the instruction and consistency that your children need, investing in other children will help your own children as well. As they watch their parents give of their time and affection to assist in unfortunate situations, it allows your children to see the gospel displayed in a tangible way that will forever impact them. It will change the way they see other children in the world. Who knows who your Timothy might be and all that he or she might do for God's Kingdom because someone took the time for him or her.

GETTING PRACTICAL

The previous passages indicate God's grand design concerning parents spiritually nurturing their children. These passages are not isolated teachings, but this theme of parental spiritual responsibility is a constant theme throughout the Old Testament and the New Testament. From the beginning, God knew that having committed parents in the home constitutes the best method for producing faithful children.

Through these scriptural mandates, parents can understand that God requires them to teach the ways of the Lord, model love for the Lord, choose to serve the Lord, and remember the works of the Lord. While children are expected to obey both parents, God expects for fathers not only to discipline their children, but also to disciple their children. Even when home situations, like Timothy's, are not ideal, God is still gracious to use maternal influences and fatherly role models to nurture young hearts.

Parental responsibility is God's chosen avenue to disciple future generations. While these biblical passages provide many practical guidelines, we will now turn to effective methods that are working to evangelize and disciple children. In the next section, we will look at elements that are working to make faith stick with the next generations.

---

[1] Walter L. Liefeld, 1 & 2 Timothy, Titus: from Biblical Text...to Contemporary Life, The NIV Application Commentary (Grand Rapids: Zondervan, 1999), 222.

[2] Donald Guthrie, The Pastoral Epistles: An Introduction and Commentary, in the Tyndale New Testament Commentaries (Leicester, England: InterVarsity, 1990), 136.

[3] Gordon D. Fee and W. Ward Gasque, 1 and 2 Timothy, Titus, New International Biblical Commentary, vol. 13 (Peabody, MA: Hendrickson Publishers, 1988), 173.

[4] Philip H. Towner, The Letters to Timothy and Titus, The New International Commentary on the New Testament (Grand Rapids: Eerdmans, 2006), 453.

[5] Margaret Davies, The Pastoral Epistles (London: Epworth Press, 1996), 61.

[6] Guthrie, The Pastoral Epistles, 135.

[7] Liefeld, 1 & 2 Timothy, Titus, 223.

[8] Thomas D. Lea and Hayne P. Griffin, 1, 2 Timothy, Titus, The New American Commentary, vol. 34 (Nashville: Broadman, 1992), 185.

[9] William Mounce, Pastoral Epistles, Word Biblical Commentary, vol. 46 (Nashville: Nelson, 2000), 471.

[10] Liefeld, 1 & 2 Timothy, Titus, 223.

[11] Mounce, Pastoral Epistles, 471.

[12] Ibid., 472.

[13] John Phillips, Exploring the Pastoral Epistles: An Expository Commentary (Grand Rapids: Kregel, 2004), 345.

[14] Liefeld, 1 & 2 Timothy, Titus, 223.

[15] Fee and Gasque, 1 and 2 Timothy, Titus, 173.

[16] Davies, The Pastoral Epistles, 62.

[17] Fee and Gasque, 1 and 2 Timothy, Titus, 173.

[18] Thomas Oden, First and Second Timothy and Titus, Interpretation (Atlanta: John Knox Press, 1989), 28.

[19] Liefeld, 1 & 2 Timothy, Titus, 226.

[20] Mounce, Pastoral Epistles, 471.

[21] Towner, The Letters to Timothy and Titus, 454.

[22] Oden, First and Second Timothy and Titus, 29.

[23] Liefeld, 1 & 2 Timothy, Titus, 229.

[24] Ibid., 30.

[25] Tate, Psalms 51-100, 289.

SECTION 2:
THE EFFECTIVE METHODS
WHAT'S WORKING WITH CHILDREN TO MAKE FAITH STICK

2

CHAPTER 8
GOSPEL ESSENTIALS

We had just begun to equip the parents in our church to evangelize and disciple their children when we came upon some conflict. Parents seemed fearful when it came to initiating spiritual conversations with their children. What I discovered was disturbing. Parents were initiating plenty of conversations with children. They were talking about standardized testing, football teams, weekday sitcoms, and a host of other topics, but talking about God scared them to death.

One father shared with me that he wasn't adequately trained to have those type of conversations with his son. I asked if he ever helped out with the son's homework in the evening. He replied, "Well, of course I do! But I've been amazed at how much I've forgotten since I was in school. I am constantly having to look up geometry hints online to help him with his homework."

As soon as he finished saying it, he gave me that look that said, "OK, you got me." Parents want the best for their children, and they are willing to do homework themselves to assist their children in any arena except in the area of spirituality. When parents struggle through awkward conversations about God, it reveals to their children that talking about God and to God must be an uncomfortable ordeal. Unfortunately, this lacking level of comfort is often passed to the next generation.

In an increasingly busy society, many forces compete against the unity of the home. In the lives of children, though, "the Church is a centripetal force. All other social forces are centrifugal."[1] That means that the church, of all institutions, should pull the family together and not segregate them. Parents should utilize the local church to assist in raising godly children. Neglecting the local church concerning a child's development is not only detrimental to the child's spiritual vitality but also exposes the parents' limited resources.[2] However, while the local church does serve to bring the family together, too many parents unfortunately rely solely upon the institution of the church to initiate faith conversations with their children.[3]

> The church, of all institutions, should pull the family together and not segregate them.

Many parents never attempt to converse with their children about God, faith, or salvation. Contrastingly, parents who have experienced spiritual harvest with their children saw their role as the "primary spiritual developers" of their children and did not expect a pastor or a church body to accomplish their assumed task of evangelism and discipleship.[4] Churches which passively comply with parental apathy create an "unhealthy dependence upon the church to relieve the family of its biblical responsibility."[5]

While initiating conversations with one's child concerning salvation can prove to be a daunting task, a concerned parent should accept this responsibility with great fervor. One study revealed, in fact, that children who had parents who took them to church but who never witnessed significant change within their parents' lives reached adulthood with a minimized view of a vital relationship with Jesus.[6] In this task, parents are the most important voice and example in the life of a child. Parents must remember that the goal is not to make a child simply spiritual but for a child to enter into a saving relationship with Jesus Christ.[7]

Above any other divine mandate for parents, God desires parents to focus their attention on producing disciples transformed by the power of the gospel. More than producing well-behaved children, God's priority is children changed from within by the message of the gospel.[8] Before communicating that message to children, a parent must convince children that their spiritual lives are important.[9] Not only are their spiritual lives important for the children's own sakes, but parents must convince their children that they personally care for their spiritual standing.[10]

Parents should create a spiritually nurturing environment within the home. They should alter the home's atmosphere to ensure that a child views choosing Christ as the most natural and anticipated decision he or she will make.[11] By creating this type of environment, parents will foster a safe haven in which a child's authentic conversion is seen as the ultimate goal.[12] In order to communicate biblical truth to their children, parents must understand the pivotal elements of the gospel message.

THE NEED FOR THE GOSPEL

Even though a child is not capable of understanding theological truths at the same level as adults, a child's conversion must be nothing less than what God expects concerning an adult's conversion. In order to be saved, children need the gospel. No matter the age, in order for a person to be saved, that person must make "a conscious turning from sin and a turning toward God (Acts 9:35; 11:34-35; 26:20)."[13] To be assured that their children are wholly converted, parents must succeed in presenting the whole gospel.

We will discuss discipleship processes, but before we can make disciples, individuals first must be converted by the power of God. When we speak of the gospel message, we are talking about the biblical truth that turns a sinner into a saint. This message is the saving power of the gospel.

Often, adults dilute the gospel message to children in order for them to understand the message. For example, many child evangelism models depict Jesus as a hero, but parents must never settle for portraying Jesus as a simple hero. He is more than a role model; he is the cornerstone of the Christian faith.[14] While certain concepts of Jesus may be easier to comprehend at different ages, parents must never dilute his true character or devalue his work.

As parents begin to teach their children, most parents will confuse their children at some time throughout this process. In attempting to educate, parents may use terms that the children cannot understand. If a parent does confuse a child, that parent should not quit but simply regroup and clarify the cloudy issue.[15]

THE MESSAGE OF THE GOSPEL

When I was in college, I learned the importance of giving a clear gospel presentation to a young person. I was the camp pastor at M-Fuge in St. Louis, Missouri during the summer when I learned this important lesson. In addition to preaching in the worship services, I would also support mission leaders during the day and invest in the lives of these students.

During an invitation one evening, a young man came down to pray with me. As we conversed, I realized that he had never experienced salvation. While the worship leader was playing behind me and students waiting in line behind him, I thought I gave him a clear picture of the gospel message. He said he understood the message and he wanted to be saved. After sharing a prayer together, we rejoiced and continued on with the rest of the worship service.

The next day, our videographer on staff went to interview him concerning what had happened the night before. At the end of the week, the staff showed the clip to the whole camp before I had a chance to view it. I was mortified!

After being asked about what happened the night before, this 13 year-old boy said, "Well, last night while we were singing, I was getting chills all over. I went up and prayed with Travis. He hugged me and said we were now blood brothers. It was awesome, man."

A version of that conversation did take place, but he walked away absorbing a very different message than I remember delivering. I am not here to judge on whether or not that night constituted a legitimate conversion experience for the boy; only God knows that. But that experience forced me do two things: 1) I went and talked with my "blood brother" to make sure he understood what happens at conversion and how it is more than getting chills and hugging a preacher, and 2) I vowed to be clearer in my presentation of the gospel, not only when sharing that message with children, but also when one day having the privilege to share that message with my own children.

While parents are blessed to experience many different events in their children's lives, no experience can compare with being with a child when he or she becomes a Christian.[16] In order to experience this event, a parent must be intentional about sharing that message with his or her child. While conversations concerning God might begin through questions posed by children, parents would be wise to initiate faith conversations themselves. Parents need to teach the message of the gospel to their children in an engaging way.[17] A parent must be clear in his or her presentation of the gospel message in order that the

> While parents are blessed to experience many different events in their children's lives, no experience can compare with being with a child when he or she becomes a Christian.

child not become confused.[18] Due to the importance of this subject, parents need to feel confident in the essentials of the gospel and the requirements for conversion. A parent must be sure of the content of the gospel before properly transmitting that information. Using an acrostic with the word "grace," the gospel's essential elements are easily memorable and transferable.[19]

The first element essential to the gospel message is the nature of *God*. Parents must teach children that "there is only one, eternal, holy, just, personal God who desires a relationship with them (Acts 17:24-31; 14:15-17)."[20] In a child's understanding about God, it is imperative that parents teach that everyone and everything has been created by this holy God, and he has ultimate say concerning how people are to live their lives.[21] This God is both holy and loving. His character is the very standard for holiness and love.[22]

The second element essential to the gospel message is the concept of *rebellion*. An individual cannot be saved until that person is aware that he or she is spiritually lost.[23] Sin is rebellion against God, and it is "any failure to conform to the moral law of God in act, attitude, or nature."[24] Parents must communicate to their children that God takes sin seriously and has real punishments associated with rebellion against him. Sin has caused mankind to lose fellowship with God.[25] Children must understand that sin is not a failure in relation to moral comparison to others, but God judges sin based upon transgression against himself.[26] While many parents desire to encourage their children by fostering a positive self image, "The central focus of childrearing is to bring children to a sober assessment of themselves as sinners....The cross of Christ must be the central focus of your childrearing."[27]

The third element essential to the gospel message is the concept of *atonement*. Atonement is what Christ had to accomplish through his life, death, and resurrection in order to provide salvation for mankind.[28] Through the person and sacrifice of Jesus, God provided atonement through a "perfect sacrificial substitute."[29] Since all rebelliously transgressed against a holy God, Christ accepted the penalty of death from sinners upon himself.[30] Parents must find a way to teach children the magnitude and the implications of what Jesus did at the cross.[31]

The fourth element essential to the gospel message is *conversion*. Conversion takes place when a person willingly responds positively to the gospel message, repents of his sin, and places trust in Christ for salvation.[32] At the point of conversion, a person must be willing to surrender, repent, and believe.[33] While the verbiage of "accepting Christ as personal savior" is popular, this phrase is not present in Scripture.[34] At conversion, a person does more than accept Jesus; that person is changed completely. To teach a child concerning salvation, parents should read their children passages about salvation and stories that convey the difference between a lost person and a reborn person.[35]

The final element essential to the gospel message is *eternal life*. Once a person is born again, Christ promises eternal life in heaven. New converts, including children, might have difficulty comprehending assurance of salvation.[36] The Bible teaches that those truly in Christ will persevere unto the end.[37] At the point of death, a person's physical body remains on earth, but one's soul enters eternity. For the believer, death brings that person into the presence of Jesus for eternity.

Salvation is all about grace (God, Rebellion, Atonement, Conversion, Eternity). It is God's grace that saved you, and prayerfully, it will be God's grace that saves your child. This gospel message should be taught and repeated to your children.

As I met with parents in our church, we realized that a church methodology principle needed to be also applied within the home. A popular church principle teaches that it is acceptable to change the medium of the gospel as long as you don't change the message of the gospel. Many people will try new approaches to getting the message across while keeping the purity of the message intact.

On the church level and within your home, the message of the gospel never changes, but the method of delivery can change. Some parents testified that a canned delivery of the gospel did not work with each child in their home. What worked with one child sometimes would have to be communicated differently with another. Evidently, it is not only wise for a parent to study the gospel but also to study the person with whom you are sharing the gospel.

SHARING YOUR TESTIMONY OF GRACE

One great way to make the gospel stick with your children is by sharing your story of how grace changed you. In sharing your testimony with your children, that doesn't mean that you must give gory details.

They don't need to be scarred for life as you recount every mistake of your past, but they might benefit to hear that Dad struggled like they struggle, and yet Jesus made all the difference.

When the Apostle Paul shared his testimony in Acts 26, he provided a great example to follow. He shared what happened before (26:4-11), during (26:12-18), and after (26:19-23) Jesus saved him. A great way to start constructing your testimony to share with your children is by following that outline.

First, what were you like before Christ (really pray concerning how much should be shared)? Second, what happened during conversion (what, when, where, why, how)? Finally, what has your life been like after that moment (how is Christ continually changing you)?

As you tell and retell your story to your children, you will be amazed at how your children will view the most pivotal figure in their lives – you (even if you don't feel like it). Your story will play a significant role in their story.

If someone interviewed your child on your conversion experience, what would they say? Start working towards your children understanding what happened before, during, and after your personal conversion experience "so that they might put their confidence in God and not forget God's works, but keep His commands" (Ps. 78:7).

It's all about grace. Not only the grace that saved you and can save your child, but it's also by God's grace that you will be able to translate that message in a clear way to your children. The Apostle Paul asked for a church to pray for his evangelistic efforts. He prayed that

God would open up a door to share the message and that he would speak in a clear manner (Col 4:3-4). If the guy who was used by God to pen the gospel message contained in the Book of Romans asked for prayer partners in order that he could share the gospel clearly, I think that is a good prayer for us as well!

What a wonderful place for parents to start. What if you ask God to open a door to share the gospel with your child? I promise that if you ask for the open door, God will swing it wide open. Will you walk through it? When the conversation starts, pray that God makes your words connect with your child. Even if your "presentation" isn't the best in the world, you trust the Holy Spirit to do what only he can do — save your child!

---

[1] George N. Luccock, The Home God Meant (New York: The Book Stall, 1922), 102.

[2] R. Kent Hughes, Barbara Hughes, and R. Kent Hughes, Disciplines of a Godly Family (Wheaton, IL: Crossway, 2004), 67-68.

[3] Alice Zillman Chapin, Building Your Child's Faith (Nashville: Thomas Nelson, 1990), 89.

[4] George Barna, Revolutionary Parenting: What the Research Shows Really Works (Ventura, CA: BarnaBooks, 2007), 56.

[5] George Barna, Transforming Children into Spiritual Champions (Ventura, CA: Regal, 2003), 81.

[6] C. Ellis Nelson, "Spiritual Formation: A Family Matter," Journal of Family Ministry 20, no. 3 (2006): 20.

[7] Robert G. Bruce and Debra Fulghum Bruce, Becoming Spiritual Soulmates with Your Child (Nashville: Broadman and Holman, 1996), 28.

[8] Tedd Tripp, Shepherding a Child's Heart (Wapwallopen, PA: Shepherd Press, 1995), xx.

[9] Rick Osborne, Talking to Your Children about God (San Francisco: Harper San Francisco, 1998), 27.

[10] Marshall Shelley, ed., Keeping Your Kids Christian: A Candid Look at One of the Greatest Challenges Parents Face (Ann Arbor, MI: Vine Books, 1990), 80.

[11] Ibid., 83.

[12] Hughes, Hughes, and Hughes, Disciplines of a Godly Family, 63.

[13] Edward L. Hayes, "Evangelism of Children." Bibliotheca Sacra 132, no. 527 (1975): 255.

[14] Bruce and Bruce, Becoming Spiritual Soulmates with Your Child, 30-31.

[15] Shelley, Keeping Your Kids Christian, 81.

[16] Benny Phillips and Sheree Phillips, Raising Kids Who Hunger for God (Tarrytown, NY: Chosen Books, 1991), 231.

[17] Sue Miller with David Stall, Making Your Children's Ministry the Best Hour of Every Kid's Week (Grand Rapids: Zondervan, 2004), 52.

[18] Hughes, Hughes, and Hughes, Disciplines of a Godly Family, 63.

[19] Timothy Beougher, GRACE: An Evangelistic Tract (Louisville: SBTS, 2004), 2. Through the work of the Billy Graham School of Missions, Evangelism and Church Growth at The Southern Baptist Theological Seminary, a gospel tract was developed using an acrostic with the word "grace" (God, Rebellion, Atonement, Conversion, Eternal Life). This gospel tract will serve as the foundation for the gospel message content communicated to parents.

[20] Will McRaney, Jr., The Art of Personal Evangelism: Sharing Jesus in a Changing Culture (Nashville: Broadman and Holman, 2003), 82.

[21] Will Metzger, Tell the Truth: The Whole Gospel to the Whole Person by Whole People: A Training Manual on the Message and Methods of God-Centered Witnessing (Downers Grove, IL: InterVarsity Press, 1981), 45.

[22] Wayne Grudem, Systematic Theology: An Introduction to Biblical Doctrine (Grand Rapids: Zondervan, 1994), 197.

[23] Hayes, "Evangelism of Children," 256.

[24] Grudem, Systematic Theology, 490.

[25] Little, How to Give Away Your Faith, 90.

[26] Metzger, Tell the Truth, 48.

[27] Tripp, Shepherding a Child's Heart, 123.

[28] Grudem, Systematic Theology, 568.

[29] McRaney, The Art of Personal Evangelism, 87.

[30] Little, How to Give Away Your Faith, 92.

[31] Rhodes, What Your Child Needs to Know about God, 17.

[32] Grudem, Systematic Theology, 709.

[33] McRaney, The Art of Personal Evangelism, 91.

[34] Metzger, Tell the Truth, 62.

[35] Ron Rhodes, What Your Child Needs to Know about God (Eugene, OR: Harvest House Publishers, 1997), 16.

[36] Metzger, Tell the Truth, 66.

[37] Grudem, Systematic Theology, 788.

CHAPTER 9
LEVELS OF LEARNING

Sarah's mom called the church office to inform the pastoral staff that Sarah was ready to be baptized. This eager mother shared with me how her daughter initiated the conversation about baptism, how she could share the most important stories concerning salvation, and how the family was very eager to get her baptized in the next few weeks. Most of the time, a call from an eager parent concerning a child's salvation is a welcomed announcement, but in this case, we were a tad guarded.

Sarah was 5.

Could God save Sarah at age 5? Absolutely. God can do anything, and after all, he's the active agent in salvation. But had God saved Sarah? That was the question that kept us very apprehensive about baptizing this young girl. We didn't want to baptize Sarah providing her family with tangible "evidence" that she was saved if she had truly not been converted. Then I struggled with the fact if God does the saving, and he is the only one who knows her heart, who am I to judge whether or not this conversion experience was legitimate?

Sarah and her mother came by the church office to schedule baptism, but one conversation with Sarah without having her mother beside her revealed some very interesting information. First, she could recite the gospel message and recite it very well. She understood key Bible stories and could relay certain biblical truths. Second, it was very obvious she was excited about the prospect of baptism.

"Sarah, I'm so impressed with all that you know about the Bible. So why is it that you want to be saved?"

"Well, Mommy says it would really make her proud and my older sister just got baptized. It was so cool when you held her under the water! She splashed a bunch of water out on my mom and then afterwards she got a lot of presents. It looked really fun!"

So, what would you do with Sarah? Additionally, what would you do with Sarah's mom? Sarah could recite all the correct information, but her motives were apparently not directed by a desire for repentance in light of her rebellious transgressions against a holy God.

While no one wants to squelch the excitement of a young child and the affirmation of a loving mother, no one also wants to give a precious child false assurance on her way to hell. I hope that phrase woke you up to what we are dealing with here. Salvation and baptism add up to more than a cute photo op. Eternity hangs in the balance.

So, how did we handle Sarah and her mother? She was never baptized at our church. We relayed our caution and reservations about baptizing Sarah to her mother, and her mother decided to find a church that would baptize her daughter. Sarah was baptized at the impressive age of 5 years old. I earnestly pray that her conversion was authentic.

In dealing with a child's salvation, we cannot be too careful. We do not want to be over zealous and give someone false assurance, but we also do not want to be too cautious and miss an opportunity when eternity hangs in the balance. Each child is different, and so a parent must learn to understand the different developmental levels that a child goes through.

> In dealing with a child's salvation, we cannot be too careful.

DEVELOPMENTAL LEVELS

Regardless of when a child is truly ready to become a Christian, parents need to start biblical education early.[1] If a parent neglects to teach a child about God, that child will entertain either misconceptions or apathetic thoughts concerning God.[2] While this task seems to overwhelm most parents due to the sensitivity and the enormity of the task, parents must remember that God is actively involved in the pursuit of children. He was reaching out to one's child before the parent started the process, and he will continue to equip a child to develop a heart and a mind for him.[3]

As children are prone to act based upon feelings, one of the parental tasks is "to minimize their feelings and encourage their faith."[4] As parents initiate faith conversations, children will learn to connect with God. Even if a home is comprised of children of differing ages, parents should still provide biblical education within the home. Parents may be surprised at what a younger child can actually comprehend concerning the gospel message.[5] Parents should realize that children are learning verbal and non-verbal lessons from the parents beginning at the time of birth, and thus it is never too early to start biblical instruction.[6]

AGE OF ACCOUNTABILITY

Much debate surrounds the issue of the age of accountability. The age of accountability is a phrase meaning that there is a time in a child's life when he or she becomes accountable to God for his or her sins. The belief holds that God would not allow a child to go to hell if that child died before he or she was able to comprehend and subsequently respond to the gospel.

When the disciples asked Jesus who was the greatest in the kingdom (Matt 18:1), he sat a child down before the disciples to answer their question (Matt 18:2). It would have been pointless for Jesus to exalt a child to hold the mantle of who belongs in the kingdom if he did not believe that a child is able to become a Christian at a young age.[7] Jesus believed in childlike faith so much that he required adults to bear a childlike resemblance in their own salvation (Matt 18:3).[8]

While an exact age of accountability is not prescribed in the Bible, statistics show that a large majority of children become Christian between the ages of six and eight.[9] Barna's research indicates that what a person believes by the age of thirteen is normally what he or she will continue to believe the rest of his or her life.[10] On the other hand, parents must be cautious even though many children do convert at an early age. For at least two centuries of its existence, the early church retained no records of allowing young children to be baptized.[11] Apparently, the first generations of Christians were at least apprehensive about rushing baptism for children.

Is there a moment in a child's life when he crosses the threshold of being responsible for his sins, or is he born responsible since he is born sinful?[12] The idea of the age of accountability originated from the tension concerning the concept of original sin. If one believes that people are born into original sin due to the curse of the Adamic nature (Rom 5:12), that person must grapple with what happens to children who die before a chance to understand or accept the gospel message.[13]

In the case of children who die at an early age, one view is that those children are secure in heaven. Due to Moses' inference that children do not know the difference between right and wrong (Deut 1:39), David's claim that he would one day see his child who had died (2 Sam 12:23), and Isaiah's prophecy of a time when a boy would understand the difference between right and wrong (Isa 7:15-16), the biblical message seems to indicate an age of accountability and a security associated with children who die before reaching that age. Since the New Testament reveals a need for personal faith for salvation, theologians developed the idea of an age of accountability in an attempt to grasp the intricacies involved with children following Christ.[14]

Some believe that the time when a child truly understands the difference between right and wrong is between 11 and 13 years of age.[15] Others believe that accountability begins when an individual child is able not only to understand when he or she has done something wrong, but also to understand the consequences of sinful actions.[16] Many scholars believe that when a child first shows indication of moral consciousness, a child is able to be converted.[17] Whatever the actual age is, an important thought for a parent to remember is to show concern over a child's spirituality without pressuring the child's decision.[18]

PROGRESSIVE LEVELS OF LEARNING

One of the first lessons parents should teach their children regarding salvation is that no one inherits salvation from one's parents and "that there are no second generation Christians."[19] Paul wrote to Timothy that from childhood he had "known the sacred writings which are able to give you the wisdom that leads to salvation through faith which is in Christ Jesus" (2 Tim 3:15). Through this statement, Paul revealed that children at some early age are able to comprehend the Scriptures and the necessary elements to becoming a Christian.[20] Due to this reality, parents should saturate a child's environment with the truths of Scripture.[21] Every parental contact with a child is shaping a child's understanding about God.[22]

When is the right time to begin initiating potential conversion conversations? Most school systems hold that six years of age is when children should begin their formal education. From this point, a child can begin to build upon those initial concepts taught during earlier years.[23] Another answer to this question is that whenever a child begins to indicate interest in matters concerning God, the time is right whether that child "is four or fourteen."[24]

Even if children are too young to comprehend the gospel fully, parents should still intentionally teach them the foundational truths of Christianity. Once a child begins to talk, parents should begin to use direct teaching concerning the existence of God.[25] Through this early teaching of the Bible, parents should desire their "children to experience now and label later."[26] The parents' primary task when teaching children from birth until the age of 4 years-old is to provide them a solid foundation of love. From this foundation, other important truths can build upon an understanding of parental love.[27]

As children grow older, they will be able to understand more about God. Children between the ages of 4 and 6 grasp a simple concept of God who is a joyful, pleasant divine being.[28] At this age, it is critical to teach children to focus upon relationships. Parents must inform children of the need for their relationship with God and with others to grow.[29]

When a child reaches the ages of 7 to 9, he is able to understand more concepts concerning God's nature, but may entertain "underlying questions, doubts, and fears."[30] During this stage, parents must commit to providing more tangible reasons for faith. As children's cognitive skills develop, parents must assure their children concerning the reliability of God's presence and character.[31] Around the age of nine, children begin to use their cognitive abilities to either confirm or deny what they have learned to this point in life.[32]

The child between the ages of 10 and 12 normally has more questions about God and is more likely to express verbal doubts concerning particular spiritual matters.[33] During this pivotal stage, parents must intentionally equip children to make wise choices according to biblical mandate. Parents must begin to move toward children independently choosing obedience to God based upon their understanding of God's commands.[34]

While children easily believe the miracles associated with Christianity, parents must reveal the reasoning behind God's miracles. When teaching children regarding the miracles of Jesus, parents must help children understand that Jesus performed these mighty acts because he truly cared for these people and not for mere display of power.[35] As children try to comprehend the cross, parents should not neglect the real meaning of that event. Parents are to educate children that Jesus desired to go to the cross to take the punishment for the sins of all people.[36] In all biblical education, parents should desire not just to transfer information, but they should also make the information personal and applicable.

As your children grow and develop, you teach them new things. All of God's Word is inspired and can benefit your children, but it's perfectly acceptable to wait and teach certain truths as your children develop. If your 3 year-old is having nightmares, you might choose to save your dragon of Revelation lesson for another day. At bedtime, I would probably refrain from explaining how the great seven-headed, red dragon was waiting on gobbling up the Christ child at his birth (Rev 12:3-4). The message is biblical and worth sharing, but share that lesson at the proper time.

When I was teaching my toddlers to memorize the 10 Commandments, I became quite a bit dumbfounded the night we arrived at commandment #7. Each previous night, I had them repeat an abbreviated version of the commandment, then I would explain what the commandment meant. "Daddy, what's 'a-donk-tree?'"

"Well, son...it means that Daddy shouldn't ever...ummm...that only me and your mother should ever...uhhh...let's start at commandment #1 again. OK?" Children need to understand the commands concerning marital faithfulness, but we have to teach it in a way they can understand it and appreciate it. When my children are 6, I may not teach them the story of David and Bathsheeba regularly. When they are 16, I will teach it to them daily! Teach the whole counsel of God, but realize that you don't have to teach it all by tomorrow.

Questions are good indicators. You will discover where your child's understanding is by the questions that he or she asks. Use your children's questions as a guide to how and what you should be teaching them. Over time, you will begin to perceive what you need to cover based upon conversations you have with them.

Remember these levels of learning as you share the gospel with them, and also remember these levels after they are saved and you disciple them in your home. Study the Scriptures and study your children to know how best to teach them. Find out what ways they learn best and utilize those methods relentlessly. Make the learning fun and engaging. If they hate school, don't make this process like their classroom. Teach in a way that is memorable and impacting.

In Christianity, we often treat someone's salvation as reaching the finish line. When a profession of faith takes place, those people closest to the individual rejoice and all resound a collective sigh of relief since the job is done. The "Get-Out-of-Hell-Free" card has been issued and we can all sleep a little bit easier tonight. Scripture paints a picture that salvation is more of a starting line than a finishing line.

> Scripture paints a picture that salvation is more of a starting line than a finishing line.

When a person is saved, he or she is justified. Justification means that the person is once and for all declared righteous in the eyes of God. After justification occurs, the next process is called sanctification, which makes the believer's life match with the declared justification. Justification saves you, and sanctification shows that you are saved. Glorification is the process when this life is over and we enter into heaven and are finally complete in every way. Even while we celebrate that the prospect of hell may be avoided at salvation, abundant life (John 10:10) is not restricted to the hereafter.

That fact is important because even when your child professes Christ, your job as a parent is not complete. As a child develops and understands more, a parent should consistently gauge the level of spiritual depth present in the child. As the child grows, assist him as he works out his salvation, "with fear and trembling" (Phil 2:12). If your child has been justified, now partner with God to help sanctify your child.

---

[1] Sally Leman Chall, Making God Real to Your Children (Tarrytown, NY: F. H. Revell Co., 1991), 147.

[2] C. Ellis Nelson, "Spiritual Formation: A Family Matter," Journal of Family Ministry 20, no. 3 (2006): 20.

[3] John T. Trent, Rick Osborne, and Kurt D. Bruner, Parents' Guide to the Spiritual Growth of Children (Wheaton, IL: Tyndale House, 2000). 104.

[4] Benny Phillips and Sheree Phillips, Raising Kids Who Hunger for God (Tarrytown, NY: Chosen Books, 1991), 245.

[5] Donald Whitney, Family Worship: In the Bible, in History and in Your Home (Shepherdsville, KY: The Center of Biblical Spirituality, 2005), 45.

[6] George Barna, Transforming Children into Spiritual Champions (Ventura, CA: Regal, 2003), 81.

[7] Ron Rhodes, What Your Child Needs to Know about God (Eugene, OR: Harvest House Publishers, 1997), 16.

[8] Edward L. Hayes, "Evangelism of Children." Bibliotheca Sacra 132, no. 527 (1975): 253.

[9] Alice Zillman Chapin, Building Your Child's Faith (Nashville: Thomas Nelson, 1990), 94.

[10] John W. Kennedy, "The 4-14 Window: New Push on Child Evangelism Targets the Crucial Early Years," Christianity Today 48, no. 7 (2004): 53.

[11] Hayes, "Evangelism of Children," 253.

[12] Wesley Haystead, Teaching Your Child about God (Ventura, CA: Regal, 1995), 105.

[13] For more information, see Millard J. Erickson's Christian Theology, 2nd ed. (Grand Rapids: Baker, 2003), 654-55.

[14] Ibid., 255.

[15] Chapin, Building Your Child's Faith, 92-93.

[16] Haystead, Teaching Your Child about God, 105.

[17] Hayes, "Evangelism of Children," 255.

[18] R. Kent Hughes, Barbara Hughes, and R. Kent Hughes, Disciplines of a Godly Family (Wheaton, IL: Crossway, 2004), 63.

[19] Ibid., 89.

[20] Rhodes, What Your Child Needs to Know about God, 16.

[21] William Sears, Christian Parenting and Child Care (Nashville: Nelson, 1991), 28.

[22] Nelson, "Spiritual Formation," 20.

[23] Chapin, Building Your Child's Faith, 92-93.

[24] Chall, Making God Real to Your Children, 148.

[25] Ibid., 21.

[26] Delia Touchton Halverson, How Do Our Children Grow? Introducing Children to God, Jesus, the Bible, Prayer, Church (Nashville: Abingdon, 1993), 48. This concept is built upon the fact that children can remember stories even if they cannot yet understand concepts. Parents should not neglect teaching children the Bible due to a child's inability to fully grasp an issue.

[27] Trent, Osborne, and Bruner, Parents' Guide to the Spiritual Growth of Children, 107.

[28] Robert G. Bruce and Debra Fulghum Bruce, Becoming Spiritual Soulmates with Your Child (Nashville: Broadman and Holman, 1996), 28.

[29] Trent, Osborne, and Bruner, Parents' Guide to the Spiritual Growth of Children, 115.

[30] Barna, Transforming Children into Spiritual Champions, 58.

[31] Trent, Osborne, and Bruner, Parents' Guide to the Spiritual Growth of Children, 121.

[32] Barna, Transforming Children into Spiritual Champions, 58.

[33] Bruce and Bruce, Becoming Spiritual Soulmates with Your Child, 28.

[34] Trent, Osborne, and Bruner, Parents' Guide to the Spiritual Growth of Children, 121.

[35] Haystead, Teaching Your Child about God, 109.

[36] Marshall Shelley, ed., Keeping Your Kids Christian: A Candid Look at One of the Greatest Challenges Parents Face (Ann Arbor, MI: Vine Books, 1990), 82.

CHAPTER 10
CHILD STEPS

I realized early on as a dad that I had unrealistic expectations concerning my children. It made no sense to me that one man-to-man conversation with a toddler was unable to produce long-lasting change. Why couldn't my reasoning skills be utilized to demand allegiance from my young, impressionable children?

I avoided much unneeded stress when I acknowledged that parenthood is a process. My goal is not to make my child a contributing member of society by age 3. My goal is to evangelize and disciple my child over the course of his or her life, but primarily over the span of a pivotal, yet limited, 18 years. Since revivals don't always spread through a home and since disciples aren't made overnight, we have to pace ourselves for the long haul.

EVANGELISTIC STEPS

When Jesus spoke to his disciples concerning evangelism and legitimate conversion, he told them a parable about a sower (Matt 13:3-9) and then later explained that parable to his disciples (Matt 13:18-23). Through this parable, Jesus taught that a person is solely responsible for sowing the seed, and the sower was not ultimately responsible for how others responded to the message. While many Christians remember this parable concerning adults who are being evangelized, parents should also remember this lesson when it comes to evangelizing their children.[1] Parents are to sow gospel seeds to the best of their ability and then trust God for the results.

Parents will passively impact their children more than any other societal force, but parents who intentionally decide to influence their children with the gospel will have greater impact on their children's lives.[2] Based on the success of churches and ministries evangelizing children, certain evangelistic principles are evident which can serve as tools for parents willing to evangelize their children. Using an acrostic for the word, "child," these five steps can assist parents in this task: chronologically teach the Bible, highlight teachable moments, initiate open-ended questions, live an authentic example, and decipher a child's readiness.

CHRONOLOGICALLY TEACH THE BIBLE

Researchers studying biblical education within the church have stated a need to develop a more thorough teaching curriculum designated for children.[3] Unfortunately, most curriculum, churches, and parents biblically educate children nonsequentially. Since children can better understand narratives, adults mainly teach children stories tragically removed out of context. Most children have understanding concerning individual stories, but they do not possess an understanding concerning the overarching story of the Bible.

In reality, most adults do not understand that overarching story of the Bible. Throughout Scripture, God revealed that biblical teaching must by systematic and not sporadic.[4] Due to this reality, the first evangelistic principle is that the greatest chance of biblical retention for children occurs if their parents teach the message of Jesus starting at creation and working through the entire biblical message chronologically.[5] To enable children to have a comprehensive understanding of the Bible and its worldview, parents should teach the entire biblical story.[6]

The parents' task is to lead children to cherish the Bible, not simply endorse the Bible.[7] Since children are able to remember stories, parents should use the biblical stories to their advantage. Instead of teaching them as isolated events, parents should start each new Bible narrative with questions allowing the child to reconstruct the preceding stories.[8] For a child truly to comprehend the biblical story, the parent must learn to connect these scriptural accounts to create a comprehensive story.[9] Through the process of teaching the Bible chronologi-

> The parents' task is to lead children to cherish the Bible, not simply endorse the Bible.

cally, a parent will be able to show a child the larger story of redemption.[10]

If a child poses a question to a parent who has no answer, that parent should never pretend to know all the right answers. As a child questions topics related to God, the parent who seeks counsel from the Bible will develop an even deeper faith because "the Word of God is robust; Christian faith can withstand close, honest scrutiny."[11] If and when a child asks questions that confound parents, parents should not indicate fear or shame but should simply attempt to find answers for the child.[12] Even if parents do not feel equipped to teach the Bible, they must realize that they simply need to stay ahead of the children. Parents who feel ill-equipped can gradually handle the totality of Scripture by preparing ahead of time.[13]

HIGHLIGHT TEACHABLE MOMENTS

While teaching the Bible chronologically, parents should never neglect to verbally communicate concerning their own personal relationship with Jesus.[14] Parents must look for opportunities to highlight teachable moments to give voice to their faith. As parents engage their children by disciplining them, giving them responsibilities, and instructing concerning respect, they should realize that all of these teachable moments should have their children's spiritual development in mind.[15]

By the time a child becomes 15 years old, that one child has asked perhaps half a million questions.[16] While parents may become annoyed by all the questions beginning with what, when, why, where, and how, intentional parents will use these opportunities to steer the conversations toward God.[17] Parents should view a questioning child as a blessing in that questions will cause the parents to do intense study in order to answer the questioning child with clarity.[18]

Because many children are prone to talking about events that transpired during their day, parents should respond to children by highlighting those teachable moments. If a child experienced conflict with a sibling, an intentional parent can illuminate that child concerning the effects of sin. Through conversations with one's child, a parent will have opportunities with a child to open a Bible to look for answers or to lead in prayer for a child's concern.[19] Parents can also use the structure of bedtime prayer for teachable moments.[20] An intentional parent will discover ways to engage his or her children with spiritual conversations regarding the events his or her children experienced throughout that day.

Even a child's sinful behavior can turn into a teachable moment. When a child sins, a mindful parent will use that opportunity to explain the spiritual ramifications for what just transpired versus simply punishing the child.[21] Parents must remember that even through discipline, they are to have the gospel as their focus. During those moments of parental correction, a parent has an opportunity to reveal not only that what a child did was wrong, but why that action was wrong in God's eyes.[22] Parents can also aid their children in understanding God's work through the Church universal. By parents educating their children concerning what God is doing around the world, children will develop a grand perception of God.[23]

Wise parents will utilize these teachable moments to guide children to truly experience a biblical truth in many different ways.[24] While highlighting teachable moments, parents must refrain from using a "one-size-fits-all" approach with their children. Every child is unique, and every process to teach each child will be unique.[25]

INITIATE OPEN-ENDED QUESTIONS

Since children are extremely impressionable, parents have a greater chance of impacting them with the gospel if a parent will simply take the initiative to prompt spiritual conversations.[26] Understanding that children are able to remember stories and retain phrases well at an early age, parents must be careful that children are understanding the gospel and not simply regurgitating the message. Children often act as if they understand adult conversation in order not to be left out when they actually are unable to understand certain concepts. Thus, parents must be aware that a child may display confidence in gospel conversations in order to impress one's parents and to appear to be wiser than that child may currently be.[27] In an attempt to gain parental approval, some children may appear to be desirous of conversion.[28] In order to ensure true change, parents must learn the discipline of asking open-ended questions.

Parents must refrain from using leading questions. Parents who ask only questions which require yes or no answers may falsely assume a child's comprehension level. If a parent asks a child, "Do you believe Jesus died on the cross for you?," that child's positive response gives little indication of actual comprehension. To avoid leading questions, parents should initiate open-ended questions which better reveal a child's understanding such as "Why did Jesus have to die on the cross?" When a child has to answer with more than a simple word or repeat a common phrase, a parent will be better able to grasp that child's real comprehension of spiritual matters.[29]

If a child prompts a conversation with a parent concerning spiritual matters, that parent should respond in such a manner that the child sees that parent's motivation and excitement. A parent could heighten a child's anticipation by telling that child to meet him or her for a special meeting since this talk is so important.[30] Once the conversation begins, a parent should ask the child why he or she wanted to talk. This open-ended question can begin to determine what is transpiring spiritually within that child.[31]

LIVE AN AUTHENTIC EXAMPLE

While intentional teaching has a significant impact upon children, studies suggest that the most important element in a child's spiritual development is parents modeling an authentic example of obedience to Christ.[32] Children struggle to maintain a genuine faith if they have parents who show lackadaisical church attendance and religious devotion.[33] For example, parents must not only teach their children that prayer is important, but they must also show their children that prayer is important by their implementation of prayer in the home.[34]   For children to take faith seriously, parents should perform some self evaluation. Parents should ascertain if they have an authentic relationship with Jesus, if that relationship is vital and growing, if Christ makes a difference in the way they live, and if that relationship can be seen outside of a church setting.[35]

Children are able to ascertain the difference between a parent's desire and a parent's obligation. A parent must check to see if he or she displays an earnest desire to attend church to commune with God or a religious obligation to appease a certain crowd of people.[36] It is unreasonable for a parent to believe that a child would possess a type of faith not witnessed within his or her own parents.[37] This approach is "pathetic when parents demand a faith or a commitment from their children that they themselves do not possess."[38]   Before Moses ever instructed parents to teach their children to love God (Deut 6:7), he taught them to love God themselves as an example for their children (Deut 6:5).[39] Just as the psalmist stated his father had told him what God had done in his life (Ps 44:1), parents should relay information to their children concerning God's activity in their own lives.[40]

The best way for a child to comprehend the power of the gospel is to hear the story of how it transformed that child's parents. No full sermon or biblical exposition is required; parents need simply to share the change Jesus made in them personally.[41] To help shape a powerful picture of God to one's children, parents should inform their children concerning pivotal moments when God intervened in their lives.[42] Through the example of holy living and the teaching of one's personal faith, a parent is able to show a child that his or her faith is genuine and tangible.

DECIPHER A CHILD'S READINESS

When a child indicates interest in becoming a Christian, parents must attempt to decipher whether or not that child is truly genuine in his or her desire.[43] While a parent may incessantly pray for and tirelessly teach for a child's comprehension of the gospel, that parent must commit never to manipulate his or her children into a forced proselytization.[44] Parents must refrain from over-anxious attempts at spiritual development, and they must learn to balance their zeal with God's sovereignty.[45] Children who are pressured by parents may have an apparent conversion without genuine assurance.[46]

Children often strive to copy their friends even in a church setting, and parents must be aware of the danger that a child's motivation for becoming a Christian could be because a friend recently became a Christian and got baptized.[47] While a family's religious involvement helps aid children to befriend other children with religious involvement and gives them a greater chance of stability and longevity within the church, conversion based on association is a serious danger.[48] For a child to be sure concerning his or her salvation, he or she must see this decision as isolated from peer or parental pressure.[49]

If a child returns from church or some event and indicates he or she was converted, the child's parents should ask the child to explain what happened as a way to assess the child's spiritual depth. A parent should not suspect that the decision was illegitimate, but that parent needs to ask questions to reveal whether that moment should be classified as conversion or as a spiritual moment without true life-changing commitment.[50] Many people who become converted at an early age often doubt that decision later in life and feel the need to recommit themselves to Christ because no one really helped them process what happened.[51]

By asking probing questions, a parent who knows the child better than the most observant pastor can discern a child's readiness and ward off the temptation to encourage a child "to pray a premature prayer."[52] A parent must avoid manipulative tactics at all costs. A parent's worst mistake could be to pressure a child "to walk the church aisle" before that child is ready.[53] In reality, a private decision can be more reliable since a public decision can confuse motives on the parents' and the child's part.[54]

If a parent deems that child ready to be converted, a parent should ask the child to pray independently in order to once again gauge the child's understanding and sincerity.[55] If a child expresses, and a parent believes, that authentic conversion has taken place, a parent must still carefully observe the child's behavior after the event. A tree is known by its fruit (Matt 7:16), and a parent should not preemptively treat a child's decision "as though his or her spiritual future is now firmly settled, but neither should the child's desire be belittled."[56]

Since children require special reassurance,[57] parents should never neglect to constantly "reinforce the assurance of salvation."[58] If a child does seem confident in his or her salvation, the parent is then responsible for affirming his or her decision and teaching that angels in heaven are actually rejoicing at that moment (Luke 15:10).[59] Once a child has been reborn, parents can help cement the reality of that experience in the mind of a child by celebrating the event. Whether a parent takes that child out to dinner, calls family members with the exciting news, or interviews the child on video to document the experience, a parent can better ensure that this event does not become lost in a plethora of childhood experiences.[60] As a child grows in Christ, a parent should continue to monitor his or her development over the years to reaffirm his or her decision.[61]

TAKE THE FIRST STEP

While the task may seem intimidating, the first requirement for parents desiring to evangelize their children is intentionality.[62] Deep, meaningful spiritual conversations do not take place by accident. The intentional parent will not only study the gospel message but will also study the child in order to proclaim the message of Jesus in the most effective manner.

Because a child's conversion is important to the parents, those parents will not rest until each of their children has turned to Jesus.[63] If parents are equipped with the necessary elements of the gospel message, they will be more apt to explain that message to their children. If parents understand the differing learning developmental levels, they will be able to understand what each child is able to comprehend. By using these evangelistic steps, parents will be able to make the most of every opportunity with their children. Parents who use these steps to explain the gospel message to a child will hopefully have the privilege to walk beside that child at the moment of conversion.

We have studied God's commands for parents, and we have looked into effective methods that are impacting homes. The biblical call is clear for parents, the tools are available to equip you on your journey. So, what are we supposed to do where the church is concerned?

If you are connected to a local congregation, and I pray that you are, more than likely, your church has programs, ministries, and maybe even staff members designated for your children. In our culture, many of our church structures are not only unbiblical, but they are impotent. They are trying to accomplish something that God never intended. It can change. A healthy union can exist between your home and your church where God is glorified and your child receives the absolute best. Are you willing to see an alternative to the status quo?

---

[1] Alice Zillman Chapin, Building Your Child's Faith (Nashville: Thomas Nelson, 1990), 95.

[2] George Barna, Transforming Children into Spiritual Champions (Ventura, CA: Regal, 2003), 59.

[3] John W. Kennedy, "The 4-14 Window: New Push on Child Evangelism Targets the Crucial Early Years," Christianity Today 48, no. 7 (2004): 53.

[4] John M. Drescher, Parents: Passing the Torch of Faith (Scottdale, PA: Herald Press, 1997), 22.

[5] Marshall Shelley, ed., Keeping Your Kids Christian: A Candid Look at One of the Greatest Challenges Parents Face (Ann Arbor, MI: Vine Books, 1990), 82.

[6] Donald Whitney, Family Worship: In the Bible, in History and in Your Home (Shepherdsville, KY: The Center of Biblical Spirituality, 2005), 37.

[7] Barna, Transforming Children into Spiritual Champions, 68.

[8] Jacobus Koelman, John Vriend, and M. Eugene Osterhaven, The Duties of Parents, Classics of Reformed Spirituality (Grand Rapids: Baker Academic, 2003), 54.

[9] Robert G. Bruce and Debra Fulghum Bruce, Becoming Spiritual Soulmates with Your Child (Nashville: Broadman and Holman, 1996), 45.

[10] While many great children's Bibles exist, I highly endorse: Sally Lloyd-Jones, The Jesus Storybook Bible: Every Story Whispers His Name (Grand Rapids: Zonderkidz, 2007) and David Helm, The Big Picture Story Bible (Wheaton: Crossway Books, 2004).

[11] Tedd Tripp, Shepherding a Child's Heart (Wapwallopen, PA: Shepherd Press, 1995), xxi.

[12] C. Ellis Nelson, "Spiritual Formation: A Family Matter," Journal of Family Ministry 20, no. 3 (2006): 21.

[13] Voddie Baucham, Family Driven Faith: Doing What It Takes to Raise Sons and Daughters Who Walk with God (Wheaton, IL: Crossway, 2007), 93.

[14] Bruce and Bruce, Becoming Spiritual Soulmates with Your Child, 32.

[15] Benny Phillips and Sheree Phillips, Raising Kids Who Hunger for God (Tarrytown, NY: Chosen Books, 1991), 232.

[16] Drescher, Parents, 24.

[17] Ibid.

[18] R. Kent Hughes, Barbara Hughes, and R. Kent Hughes, Disciplines of a Godly Family (Wheaton, IL: Crossway, 2004), 66.

[19] Sally Leman Chall, Making God Real to Your Children (Tarrytown, NY: F. H. Revell Co., 1991), 156.

[20] Ibid., 160.

[21] Koelman, Vriend, and Osterhaven, The Duties of Parents, 53.

[22] Tripp, Shepherding a Child's Heart, 123.

[23] Phillips and Phillips, Raising Kids Who Hunger for God, 237.

[24] Barna, Transforming Children into Spiritual Champions, 87.

[25] George Barna, Revolutionary Parenting: What the Research Shows Really Works (Ventura, CA: BarnaBooks, 2007), 42.

[26] Barna, Transforming Children into Spiritual Champions, 59.

[27] Wesley Haystead, Teaching Your Child about God (Ventura, CA: Regal, 1995), 107.

[28] Edward L. Hayes, "Evangelism of Children." Bibliotheca Sacra 132, no. 527 (1975): 257.

[29] Haystead, Teaching Your Child about God, 115

[30] Chapin, Building Your Child's Faith, 97.

[31] Hayes, "Evangelism of Children," 260.

[32] Barna, Transforming Children into Spiritual Champions, 84.

[33] George N. Luccock, The Home God Meant (New York: The Book Stall, 1922), 98.

[34] Chall, Making God Real to Your Children, 158.

[35] Phillips and Phillips, Raising Kids Who Hunger for God, 234.

[36] Chall, Making God Real to Your Children, 153.

[37] Hughes, Hughes, and Hughes, Disciplines of a Godly Family, 60.

[38] Ibid., 62.

[39] William Sears, Christian Parenting and Child Care (Nashville: Nelson, 1991), 27.

[40] Phillips and Phillips, Raising Kids Who Hunger for God, 233.

[41] Bruce and Bruce, Becoming Spiritual Soulmates with Your Child, 39.

[42] Phillips and Phillips, Raising Kids Who Hunger for God, 234.

[43] Ibid., 246.

[44] Hughes, Hughes, and Hughes, Disciplines of a Godly Family, 64.

[45] Hayes, "Evangelism of Children," 258.

[46] Karl Graustein with Mark Jacobsen, Growing Up Christian (Phillipsburg, NJ: P&R Publishing, 2005), 33.

[47] Phillips and Phillips, Raising Kids Who Hunger for God, 246.

[48] Blake J. Neff and Donald Ratcliff, Handbook of Family Religious Education (Birmingham, AL: Religious Education Press, 1995), 46.

[49] Shelley, Keeping Your Kids Christian, 83.

[50] Chall, Making God Real to Your Children, 148.

[51] Hayes, "Evangelism of Children," 256.

[52] Phillips and Phillips, Raising Kids Who Hunger for God, 247.

[53] Chapin, Building Your Child's Faith, 95.

[54] Hayes, "Evangelism of Children," 259.

[55] Ibid., 260.

[56] Haystead, Teaching Your Child about God, 117.

[57] Shelley, Keeping Your Kids Christian, 85.

[58] Chapin, Building Your Child's Faith, 98.

[59] Ron Rhodes, What Your Child Needs to Know about God (Eugene, OR: Harvest House Publishers, 1997), 18.

[60] Phillips and Phillips, Raising Kids Who Hunger for God, 248.

[61] Shelley, Keeping Your Kids Christian, 84.

[62] Barna, Revolutionary Parenting, 34.

[63] Chapin, Building Your Child's Faith, 89.

SECTION 3:
THE HEALTHY UNION
WHAT HAPPENS WHEN THE HOME AND THE CHURCH COLLIDE

3

CHAPTER 11
THE PARADIGM SHIFT

At North Side, we were concluding the bulk of this research and wrapping up our final training sessions for parents when a parents' meeting was called. We only call meetings for major items. Our elders were presenting their recommended candidate for our student pastor position.

We had recently gone through a time of transition in that ministry, and one of our own had stepped into the interim role. Ben had served as a discipleship group leader for teenagers, and while we searched for God's man to lead this ministry, Ben had agreed to help out. As we searched, God revealed to us that he had already found the right guy — and that this "right guy" was already serving in that position!

In the parents' meeting, we explained that we had gone through numerous résumés and interviewed many candidates only to be reassured that God had his hand on Ben for this position. The selection was not only met with approval, but we had parents rejoicing and saying they had been praying that Ben could take the job full-time.

The meeting appeared to be winding down to a conclusion when one parent raised a concern. How would our church's student ministry be impacted when Ben and his wife, Christina, had children in their own home? The parent's concern was valid. In their stage of life, this godly, young couple had plenty of time to invest in the students in our church. The addition of children into their home would rightfully take away time and attention from the students in the church.

On the other hand, many churches think it is preposterous to hire a student pastor when he has *not* raised students of his own. The hesitancy has been expressed this way — "How can he raise our kids when he hasn't raised his own?" That question touches on a central issue — we didn't want to hire anyone to raise our kids. At our church, we wanted something completely different.

I was wiggling in my seat, unsure if I needed to address the concern, when someone else took care of it. Another parent stood up and calmly yet passionately stated, "I hear your concern, but it isn't Ben's job to raise my kids. That's my job. He's here to support us, not the other way around."

Sitting in my chair, notes nestled in my lap from teaching parents, literally moments earlier, to evangelize their children I began to feel the tears stream down my cheeks. God had done it. We had just experienced the paradigm shift in our church for which we had been praying.

Since the inception of student ministry (not that many years ago), the growing belief is that parents should aid and assist the student pastor to evangelize and disciple the students. By either serving in assistant teaching roles or handling crowd control, parents are expected to help the student pastor in his ministerial work focused on their children. I cannot begin to tell you how many parents describe that situation and say that the student pastor spiritually "raised my child."

If we were to follow the biblical example, we would reverse the trend. Parents should not aid and assist the student pastor. The student pastor should aid and assist parents to evangelize and disciple their own children.

At this point in the conversation, it would be wise to see what the role of a pastor is actually supposed to be. God appoints leaders to "equip the saints for the work of ministry, for building up the body of Christ" (Eph 4:12). Did you catch that? Ministers are not supposed to do the work of ministry. Ministers are supposed to equip the congregation to do the work of ministry!

As God had been leading us on this journey of equipping parents, we were sure of one thing: we would not hire anyone to raise our members' children. Why would we hire someone to do the job that God expected parents to do? We wanted our next student pastor to be a second, supportive voice in a child's life, affirming what the parents were

> Why would we hire someone to do the job that God expected parents to do?

already teaching. This pastor would help show teenagers that their parents weren't crazy as he backed up the instruction that was given in the home.

In addition to being a biblical paradigm shift, it was wise as well. The majority of student and children's ministries as we know them do not work. They are producing lackluster results.

During the Jesus Movement of the early 1970s, Southern Baptist churches baptized 138,000 teenagers. This great harvest led many churches and parachurch organizations to hire youth ministers to capitalize on the growing movement. Since that time, the number of youth and children's ministers has dramatically increased while baptism numbers have declined sharply. 35 years after this great harvest, 50% of all Southern Baptist churches did not have one youth baptized in their congregation within the previous year. There are more workers and programs geared towards young people than ever before and yet fewer recorded salvations and baptisms.[1] Something is seriously wrong with that picture.

THE ROLE OF THE CHURCH STAFF

If we throw all of our preconceived notions out the window concerning a church staff, what is left? The role of church leaders in the Bible, as mentioned above, was to equip the saints for the work of ministry, not to do all the work of the ministry. In fact, think how misplaced the word "staff" is when it comes to the New Testament church. I'm not saying that churches shouldn't have paid staff members (I'm a "staff member" myself), but we should be careful not to form the church, a body of believers, into an American corporate model.

The biblical role of elders is not to be a board of advisors. They are meant to be shepherds. They are to teach, protect, lead, and care for the needs of a congregation. At our church, we have staff elders and non-staff elders, but we all understand that shepherding God's people is a full-time job. As our congregation has grown, we have called more elders into service. We have an elder, or a pastor, spiritually responsible for approximately 100 people. While that is a fairly manageable ratio, that is still too large of a group to care for and minister to each person specifically. In order to care for a church well, elders must equip other leaders to maintain relationships with the entire congregation.

An elder can adequately care for a group of people, but if he doesn't care for one particular group of people, he is disqualified from service. Specifically, if a man neglects to care for his family, he is unfit for Christian leadership and service. The Apostle Paul states that "if anyone aspires to the office of overseer, he desires a noble task" (1 Tim 3:1). It is a high calling but with that high calling comes serious qualifications.

"Therefore an overseer must be above reproach, the husband of one wife, sober-minded, self-controlled, respectable, hospitable, able to teach, not a drunkard, not violent but gentle, not quarrelsome, not a lover of money. He must manage his own household well, with all dignity keeping his children submissive, for if someone does not know how to manage his own household, how will he care for God's church?" (1 Tim 3:2-5).

While many qualities must be present in an overseer, two of them focus on the home.

First, this leader must be the husband of one wife. While this phrase is widely debated, it is most often understood to mean that he is committed to his present wife. The Greek phrase literally reads, "of one woman man." Listed before his abilities to teach, an elder must be a man who takes care of the needs of his wife and is wholly committed to her.

Second, this spiritual leader must be able to keep his children in check in the way he manages the house. If he can't keep his own children in line, how will he be able to keep other members of the church in line? A pastor should be able to corral his children into obedience. That phrase does not expect perfect, sinless children, but it does expect a father who is not allowing sin to go unnoticed or unaddressed.

Our culture has a stereotype of pastors' children that is the complete opposite of this biblical expectation. When people mention a "preacher's kid," they are normally referencing some rebellious hellion bent on tarnishing his father's reputation in the community. That stereotype reveals more than an unfortunate circumstance, it shows unbiblical perspectives and qualifications present in the church today.

Repeatedly, many "preacher's kids" reveal a father who took care of the needs of everyone else in the church at the expense of those in his own house. In attempts to appease a certain member or a certain family, he neglected his own wife and children. As the years went by, not only does the minister's family resent the man of the house, but they also resent the church the took away the man of the house. Many may leave the institution, never to return.

Your pastors need to care for their own children more than they care for your children. The biblical model is for a pastor to care for his wife, his children, and then to equip the saints for the work of the ministry. By his teaching and through his example, he can show you how to evangelize and disciple your children because he is doing the same thing within his own family.

Your pastor cannot fix every marriage in the church. He needs to nurture his own. He cannot fix all of your children's issues because he is trying to keep his own children from wandering away from God.

A church needs to have high expectations for its ministers, but it needs to ensure that they are God's high expectations and not unrealistic manmade expectations. God wants men in the gospel ministry who are fulfilling their callings, and a church needs to allow its pastors to be obedient to God more than anything else. You need to give your ministerial leadership room to take care of their families.

Frankly, your pastor might be needed more at his son's soccer game than beside your hospital bed. I am not saying that a pastor should not do hospital visitation or pastoral counseling, but if he answers the call of every need in a given congregation, he is unable to care for his family and therefore unfit to lead that congregation anymore. Every church wants the best

> If your pastor answers the call of every need in the congregation, he is unable to care for his family and therefore unfit to lead that congregation anymore.

pastor they can find. Make sure that once you find him you don't disqualify him by not allowing his focus to be on his own home.

THE ROLE OF CHURCH PROGRAMMING

Church programming should not be glorified babysitting. If the job of ministers is to equip the saints, then church programming should seek to accomplish the same task. In our society, parents can become chauffeur services shuttling children from one activity to the next, but the church should not be an additional extracurricular activity. The church is God's chosen vehicle to bring hope to the world — it is not the community recreation center.

A church program should have more purpose than to fill a hole in the calendar or to provide daycare while parents are involved in a church group. At North Side, we don't believe that all programs are evil. We do concern ourselves with more than just leading weekend worship services. We understand, however, why churches move away from family programming.

We do not believe that all programs are evil, but we do think unintentional programs are evil. If you are going to provide a program, it should count for something. Do not copy the program of the church down the street either. Dedicate your church to fulfilling God's expectations and do not fall prey to church territorial competition.

In children's and youth ministries, do not replace parents — supplement parents. Aid and assist your church's most qualified evangelists and disciple makers to do what they are uniquely qualified to do — raise up the next generation for Christ! Don't allow anything on the church calendar that doesn't aid and assist the obedience of the Great Commission within your church members' homes.

Concerning the programs for parents, make sure that they are freed up to spur one another on to love and good deeds (Heb 10:24-25). The title you give this process is irrelevant. It doesn't matter if it is a Sunday School or a small group. Make sure you allow parents to meet with other parents in such a way that equips them to become disciple makers in their home. Co-ed groups are helpful because they unite the husband and wife. Separate men's and women's groups allow for more transparency and honesty. At our church, we allow both models and see fruit in both. Ensure that the curriculum is not so lengthy that the parents don't have time to discuss how to apply the information. It is important to hear the Word, but make sure to allow time for applying the Word as well (James 1:22).

In the course of a church year, it is impossible to do parenting classes all the time with other needs simultaneously present. As you calendar, plan for training events periodically. Make resources available throughout the year so that, even if a parenting sermon series is not planned, your parents have a wealth of information to equip them to disciple their children.

Concerning the programs for students and children, create biblical, quality programming that supports what is happening in the home. In an ideal situation, every parent in your church will be discipling every child in your church. The role of church programming will be to support and supplement that instruction. Understanding that every church is far from that ideal situation, leadership will need to include periodic gospel presentations and constant biblical, doctrinal, and practical age-appropriate teaching that equips the children to follow God.

As church leadership charts the direction as far as teaching the next generations, give attention to the big picture without neglecting the immediate needs. Situations will arise in your church and community that call for a sudden shift in direction concerning weekly teachings, but for the most part, leaders should know exactly what they are aiming for concerning biblical instruction.

Realizing that children come through ministries for a given amount of time, plan accordingly. Imagine if a child would walk into your children's programming in first grade, what would you want him or her to know, comprehend, and be able to do by the time they left the fifth grade? If a middle schooler never missed a Sunday in your church, what would you want him or her to understand? When a senior in high school graduated, and if he or she never missed a program your church did, where would the student be spiritually?

The beauty about long-term planning is twofold: 1) it makes churches look at the big picture, and 2) it allows itself to be repeated every few years which saves money, resources, and time since you don't have to recreate teaching guides year after year. Of course, each church should constantly evaluate how they teach, but what they teach shouldn't change that much. It's a given that each church will need to focus on the gospel year after year with children.

At North Side, our strategy is to teach the Bible chronologically to our 4 and 5 year-olds. Through a rotation, one year is dedicated to studying major stories of the Old Testament and the next year is dedicated to studying major stories of the New Testament. Our elementary aged children continue to learn the Bible chronologically but begin to pull out additional biblical principles along with those stories to allow for deeper understanding and application. During the teenage years, we use seven student essentials to serve as categories to guide our biblical teaching (our essentials use the acrostic "student" to help us remember: Secure faith, Trustworthy relationships, Unwavering obedience, Doctrinal understanding, Educated worldview, Necessary tools, True service). Everything is intentional.

THE OTHER ROLE

We strive to make our ministry programs, or "environments," as quality as possible. These environments serve as a place to build relationships where we can further disciple people. Our goal is to disciple parents through worship, small groups, and service groups so that they can go home and disciple their children more effectively.

In our environments for children and students, we always seek to be engaging and fresh without ever compromising the biblical mandates. We do not want to enable the upcoming generation of church leaders to think that the church's goal is to meet their expectations or make each week more flamboyant than the week before in order to keep them coming. The call of a Christian is to come and die. We do not want to use a "bait and switch" approach for them or their parents. That's why we don't attempt to meet everyone's preferences. First, that is absolutely impossible. Second, we don't want to lure them in with an approach that communicates it's all about them, and then, once we have them, we tell them it's now time to die to self and it's not about them anymore. That's not only unwise, it's misleading.

In order to do that, we constantly have to disciple our church to remember that the building and activities are not the only places and times when God only meets with his people. We will pray, plan, and work very hard to make sure our church programs are great. We will expect our staff members to be in the absolute best spiritual state you could possibly imagine, but at the end of the day, our best attempts will be to serve as a catalyst for home discipleship. The other role in this partnership is parents. Partnering with the church will allow parents to disciple their children around the family altar.

---

[1] Tammi Reed Ledbetter, "Better equipped than ever but less effective," accessed 9 September 2011 [on-line]; http://www.texanonline.net/special-reports/better-equipped-than-ever-but-less-effective.

CHAPTER 12
THE FAMILY ALTAR

    My wife and I decided to do something foolish: we put our house up for sale with a couple of 2 year-old boys living under our roof. The mentality concerning your living conditions changes when you know that a sudden phone call could mean someone wants to come and look inside your house. During these months, our boys grew weary of the song, "Clean up, clean up, everybody clean up. Clean up, clean up, do your part."

    One Sunday evening, we were relaxing at the house after a full day with our church family. My cell phone rang, and a prospective buyer was interested in looking at the house. "Sure, we would love for you to come by. When would be a good time for you?"

    "We could be there in 15 minutes."

    "15 minutes? Sounds great! See you then."

As I hung up the phone, the look in my wife's eyes was not as excited as I had anticipated as she eavesdropped upon my side of the conversation. Since the day had been very busy, we had left some chores unfinished around the house that we had planned on getting to tomorrow. As a mad dash of cleaning commenced, I repeatedly reminded her as we would fly past each other in the hall, "You'll thank me when the house sells."

"For your safety, you better hope it sells," she reminded me.

By the time the couple arrived minutes later, the house was in great condition. The couple loved it, but unfortunately for my personal well-being, they passed on buying it. While we laughed later about the boys' fascination with our spastic behavior during our cleaning spree, I was reminded that the two of us have different standards of what clean is in a house. I have one standard that I believe is clean. My wife says what I believe to be "clean" is what she labels as "straightened." Her standard is much higher than mine.

It made me think about how God views what happens in our home. Not the cleanliness of our rooms per se, but how does God see the holiness of our hearts? It is easy for any parent to think he or she is successful because the home is not as dysfunctional as the one he or she remembered from childhood. I know we can all find homes on our streets that are filled with more issues than fill our own homes, but our standards are way off from God's standards. If God paid a visit to your home, would you pass his inspection?

INSPECTING THE HOME

As our church began to mobilize parents to evangelize and disciple their children, I assembled a focus group of parents to obtain differing perspectives. They brought helpful insights into the project's findings, such as how their parents were involved in their own spiritual development, how they had seen successes and failures in their own home, and what type of training had prepared them to become evangelists. While these parents did confirm their passion for evangelizing and discipling their own children, they also did not deny fear associated with their own inabilities.

They easily empathized with parents who felt unqualified for the job, but these parents were not shrinking back from their responsibility. Their insight into the fears of most parents proved to be helpful as I crafted the upcoming sermon series at our church. As the first meeting concluded, I gave them a focus group questionnaire (Appendix 5) and asked them to complete it before we reconvened the following week.

The three couples, my wife, and I gathered together six weeks later to discuss our answers to the provided questions. Out of the eight people in this group, only one person was converted in the presence of her parents. While this member was thankful for the experience, she vividly remembered that she was doing more of the questioning, and her parents really never took any initiative with her concerning faith conversations.

While the degree of parental involvement varied from person to person, all group members wished their parents would have been more intentional with their spirituality. Many of the stories involved a parent's taking the child to church but never displaying a personal devotion for the child to observe. Certain group members indicated that their parents encouraged moral behavior apart from the biblical reasoning behind morality.

Through the remaining discussion, key items emerged. First, the parents were concerned they were going to force Christianity on their children. Since their own parents had not been intentional enough, these parents were worried they might overemphasize obedience to the Lord so much that it would cause their children to rebel into prodigal status. Interestingly, no one in that group said that his or her own parents did enough, but they had always heard people warn about not forcing religion on their children. In this group's knowledge, they had never encountered someone who had walked away from the faith due to authentic followers of Jesus who had been intentional with their children.

They could count many people who walked away from the church whose story was a home led by parents devoted to religious institutions, but whose home was devoid of any significant change. Church attendance minus real change resulted in straying children. Consistent followers of Jesus typically produced another generation of consistent followers of Jesus.

> Church attendance minus real change resulted in straying children.

Second, the uniqueness of each child within a home was noted. One father of post-elementary aged children noted that he had raised all three of his children in the same manner, and each of them was displaying differing levels of Christian devotion. Due to this discussion, I noted that it is important for parents not only to study the gospel, but also to study intently the individual child they are evangelizing. A packaged presentation will not succeed equally with each child. A parent must study his or her child to know how to present the gospel uniquely since each child's needs and understanding are unique, but a wise parent will make the most of every opportunity presented with that child (Col 4:6).

THE FAMILY ALTAR

Intentionality is key concerning family discipleship. One way to be intentional is to have regular times of worship together as a family. I am not talking about when a family goes to a church campus together. That event is important and pivotal, but I am speaking of when a family gathers together within the home for the sake of growing in Christ. I am talking about times in your home without access to a staff member, pipe organ, or Sunday School quarterly. I'm talking about what could happen when you, a Bible, and your family could collide.

In a time when few families watch TV together, eat a meal together, or share a Saturday playing together, the thought of worshiping together seems like a far-fetched goal. Our culture bombards us with the notion that children need to be independent and have room to develop on their own. Children use the overstated line that their friends get certain privileges and so they should be privy to them as well. What transpires is family members isolating themselves in different rooms in the home without any discipling interaction taking place.

If you think your children would balk at the thought of your family gathering together at a family altar for worship on a regular basis, then that is all the more urgent of a reason to start this practice.

The term "family altar" speaks to a time when the leader of the home gathers the family together to focus on God. For some families, that may mean once a week. It could be Sunday evening as the family prepares for another week. It could be Saturday evening as they family prepares their heart for worship with their church the next morning. Other families might practice it everyday at the breakfast table or during nighttime prayers.

Why is the family altar important? God says so – that's why! As a reminder, here are just a few of the examples of God's stance on the family altar: Abraham was told to teach his children so that following generations would know the Lord (Gen. 18:19). Moses taught that parents were to teach their children to love the Lord all throughout the day (Deut. 6:7). The psalmist taught the necessity of God's people declaring God's greatness to the next generations (Ps. 78:3-7). Solomon taught that if you trained a child in the Lord, they would not depart from that way (Prov. 22:6). Fathers were instructed to teach children in the instruction of the Lord (Eph. 6:4).

What should you do when together? First, get in the Bible together. If you don't know the Bible that well, just stay one step ahead of your children. You will learn it better as you teach it to them. At differing ages, you might use children's Bibles, but it is very helpful to read chronologically. Often children are only taught stories devoid from context and they don't see the big picture. We recommend resources like *The Big Picture Storybook Bible* or *The Jesus Storybook Bible*. If your church has a reading plan or is studying a book, that is another great option.

Second, spend some time in prayer. Don't rush through this, and get creative with it. Ask for prayer requests from your family. Get in a circle and have each person pray for the person on the right. Have a set prayer focus for each day (Sunday – church staff, Monday – friends, etc.). Use this time to work on any family dynamics that need the Lord's guidance.

Third, make some time to worship together through music. Even if you don't play an instrument or think you can sing well, you can lead your family in musical worship. You could sing a cappella or along with a CD. If you do have a family musician, stir up that gift in him or her (2 Tim. 1:6).

Don't expect the church or another person to do what God has called and equipped you to do! Disciple your family. You might feel squeamish at the thought of it right now because you feel disqualified. Fears of failure might keep you from ever making the first attempt. Just like every other man and woman who ever attempted something for God, mistakes will be made. The greater mistake would be never to try in the first place.

On a certain Spring evening, I took off early to do something special with the Agnew boys. The weeknights had been pretty hectic, and I was worried I had not spent enough time with my sons. Some of the guys in our college Bible study played on Lander's baseball team, and so I decided attending one of their games would be a great, manly trip for us. We had been playing a lot of baseball in the yard at that time, and I thought the game would surely mesmerize the boys.

After loading the boys in the truck and finding our way to the field, I realized something about taking two almost 3 year-olds to a baseball game: it's a horrible idea.

The game was great, but that age was not the ideal age to sit down on bleachers and watch a baseball game in which we were not participants. After the excitement associated with the first hit, the boys resorted to picking up old peanut shells and throwing them on people in front of us. Foul balls were whizzing past our heads, and I was jumping up on my healing broken ankle to knock balls away from my sons' unsuspecting frames. I felt like I was herding cats just to keep them near me and away from oncoming danger.

By the time we got to the truck, we had two snotty noses, two bloody knees, a dad with a backache and a sore ankle, dirty hands, a band-aid, pollen-stained "Cool Like Dad" shirts, and two foul balls.

What was wild was everyone told me earlier that day how sweet it was that the three of us were going to the baseball game. After the game, as I relived the game's events, everyone I came into contact with stated, "Yeah, I didn't think they were going to sit still and watch the game at that age." I really would have appreciated those insights before we went!

Lesson learned? You bet. Even though it wasn't the ideal outing for a father and his sons, at least it was an outing. At least we got in the truck with a memory and some souvenirs. At least I made an effort during a busy week to connect with my sons.

Parents, it's better to attempt than to regret. You won't choose all the right things, but when you choose to make time for your children, it will always be the best thing. When you choose to get intentional with their spiritual development, it will always be a good thing even if you don't have a perfect track record.

> Parents, it's better to attempt than to regret.

While baseball games, vacations, and camping trips are memory-making events in a family's life, they will never ever replace what could happen when a family decides to worship together. Nothing can compare to the impact on the next generation when parents intentionally gather the family around God's Word. Out of all the memories made in one's childhood, none could have more eternal significance than when a family rallied together to make much of God.

FAMILY WORSHIP GUIDES

As mentioned earlier, the role of ministers are to equip the saints for the work of ministry (Eph 4:12). We do expect our parents to lead their families in worship, but we partner with them by providing family worship guides to equip the parents for this endeavor. Many approaches exist for how to equip families for time spent at the family altar. Like many other churches, we provide parents with information concerning what their children have learned in church programming they have attended.

In addition, we provide weekly family worship guides that correspond with what we are focusing on together as a church body.

On Thursdays, I post a family worship guide that any family, regardless of size or context, can utilize before Sunday morning's services in order to worship together. Some families do it on Saturday nights. Some families gather around the breakfast table on Sunday morning. Others go out to the park on an afternoon. It is a simple guide that is adaptable to different family situations.

The content is focused on preparing the hearts of individual families to gather together with their church family. Psalm 100:4 states, "Enter his gates with thanksgiving, and his courts with praise! Give thanks to him; bless his name!" Did you catch that? We are not supposed to enter the gates of our church buildings and then start the worship. We are supposed to enter in *with* worship! That distinction makes a huge difference! We are not supposed to arrive in a befuddled state hoping the pastor will get our attention and lead us to worship. We are supposed to gather together with praise already pouring from our lips!

My goal in providing family worship guides is for families to quiet their hearts before God before ever arriving on the church campus. Imagine what your next worship service could be like if everyone entered in worship rather than rushing in the last moment trying to find a seat? What would happen if families were not running around trying to get everyone dressed and presentable for a program and instead focused upon the receptiveness of their hearts? Change would begin to happen!

My process for writing the family worship guides begins with the Bible. I focus the content on the passage of Scripture upon which the church's sermon will be based. From that passage, I attempt to "set the table" for the message and the time of worship. How could this time spent as a family prepare them for worship as a church family? How could this time bring them closer as a family? What could God's Word teach them during this time?

When we started teaching through the Book of John on Sunday mornings, I wanted to provide Bible study and worship that would give any needed background information on the upcoming passage. When the sermon was based upon John 1:1-14, the passage on Jesus being the Word and the light sent from God, I equipped parents to see the connection with other biblical passages.

In the "Discover" section, I gave an optional activity where families could use flashlights in a dark room or outside at night to navigate the family's path. As a family discussed the benefit of that light in a dark place, they then began to talk about how Jesus came as a light to illuminate this dark world.

In the "Study" section, we encouraged families to read the creation account in Genesis 1 to see the similarities between God creating physical light in Genesis and God bringing about spiritual light through the person of Jesus in John 1. In the "Pray" section, we challenged families to pray for an unreached people group with which our church has a relationship. Our prayers focused upon that people seeing the light of Jesus. We also prayed that Jesus' light would shine in our own homes.

To conclude the time together, I also provided a "Worship" section. With this message, Tim Hughes' song, "Here I Am to Worship" was a great family worship song. I provided a chord chart for anyone who could play an instrument in the home. For those homes without musical instrumentalists, I also embedded a YouTube video with that song accompanied by lyrics. Many weeks, I provide a new worship song that we might be singing as an entire congregation in a way to inform our church concerning the story behind a song or to introduce it to our members. It's neat to watch a new song not be new to everyone as you can tell families have worshiped together to it the night before.

With each family worship guide, I remind parents that it is simply that: a guide. It can be changed. Adaptation is absolutely acceptable. It surely can be improved. The point is for it to serve as a simple guide. Parents have been thrilled to have a resource to equip them. Children have been excited about the time each week. Teenagers have actually emailed me thanking me for these guides because it is bringing their families closer together.

A true partnership between a church and a family can exist with family worship guides. Church leadership provides direction and equips the saints for the work of the ministry, and parents do their part of the ministry by ministering to the children in their home. A tragic omission in the church happens today not always because people don't do what they are called to do, but because they simply don't know *how* to do what they are called to do. With church leadership providing the tools parents need, the next generation can be adequately discipled within the home.

With family worship guides, pastors and/or leaders can begin to equip their parents to be preachers, teachers, and worship leaders of the tiny worshipers in their home. I don't know if we can truly comprehend what could happen in a church if the parents began to rally their families around the family altar. I might not be able to comprehend it, but I sure would like to experience it. And for this invaluable end I will strive, not only for my own home, but for all the homes of our church family.

CHAPTER 13
EQUIPPING PARENTS

    Early on in marriage, I realized the need my wife had to feel safe and secure. As I studied Scripture, I realized that God wanted me to provide her with emotional, spiritual, financial, and physical security. I began to study how my wife felt secure, and I tried to adapt my life to bestow that feeling of comfort for her.

    In this process, I also realized how different we were. When we first got married, we lived in a somewhat rough area with some very suspect neighbors. No insurance agent in town would provide us insurance due to the nighttime activities transpiring within the neighborhood. It was a regular occurrence that sometime during the night, Amanda would poke me under the covers alerting me to a suspicious sound outside. I would search for any impending danger, reassure her that everything was safe, and I would try to drift back to sleep.

When the sounds became more frequent outside our house, I turned into a carefree optimist in order to get some much needed shuteye. Amanda would abruptly sit up in bed and ask, "Did you hear that?"

Usually, I had not heard whatever "that" was. I *had* been fast asleep. Over time, I began to collect quite the list of possible noisemakers to ease my bride's troubled mind. Once she noticed that I had a revolving door of answers for her concerns, her sense of security began to waver. She was wise enough to know that the sounds can't always be the wind, a car door, or the neighbor's chihuahua.

One night, that all changed. We both sat up in bed one evening alarmed by a loud crash in the kitchen. From our vantage point, we could see the reflection of the backdoor glass move rapidly across the wall of our kitchen indicating that our back door had just been opened abruptly. Amanda whispered, "Trav, somebody's in the house!"

At the point in which I would normally reassure her, I looked at her in the eyes and replied, "Yep."

"You really think someone is in the house? You always tell me it's OK, and now you think someone is out there. What are you going to do?"

As I slowly eased at of bed, I replied, "Say 'hello' to whoever is in our kitchen."

"Trav, this is serious! What are you going to do? You don't have anything to protect yourself with!"

Had I been in a calmer state of mind, I would have replied with some clever zinger concerning my impressive physical physique or combative ninjutsu skills that would have calmed all of her fears. Instead of talking about it, I simply prepared my stance for possible, impending ruckus and eased myself around the corner hoping to make a light snack out of whoever was in my kitchen. Thankfully, no one was waiting for me there. The wind storm and a malfunctioning deadbolt caused the late night scare, and our home was safe and secure once I collected all of our laundry that had fallen out the door and down the steps.

One thing I did learn about myself that night: no one was going to get to my family without having to go through me first. While my masculinity is reluctant to admit I was fearful that night, I at least can confidently say that if danger comes, I will stand up to it. I may not be the most capable man in many areas, but I am the most capable man to protect my home. No one cares about the people in it more than I do.

FIGHT FOR YOUR FAMILY

When Nehemiah led a group of exiled Israelites to rebuild the wall of Jerusalem, he probably never anticipated the level of resistance that he would face. Opposition came at them from every side. As enemies conspired against the progress (Neh 4:7-8), Nehemiah had to protect God's people without an army.

Nehemiah was forced to rely on men with varying levels of military prowess. In a stunning move, Nehemiah places every able man in the exposed places of the wall and tells them to fight. In order to obtain the ferociousness needed to win the battle, Nehemiah placed every man near his clan as the last line of defense before the enemy could reach that man's family (Neh 4:13). Before the battle began, Nehemiah reminded the people, "Do not be afraid of them. Remember the Lord, who is great and awesome, and fight for your brothers, your sons, your daughters, your wives, and your homes" (Neh 4:14). In this holy moment, God's people obtained victory through the hands of some fathers who held the line and refused to let any threat past them and endanger their families.

A military power may not attempt to breach the walls of your house, but make no mistake, an enemy is on the attack. Satan is described as a "roaring lion, seeking someone to devour" (1 Pet 5:8). His plan is to "steal and kill and destroy" (John 10:10). An enemy is most definitely lurking around your home, how committed are you to fight him? How precious to you are the people in your home? What will you do to ensure that they are safe under your oversight and care?

If the goal is not to drop your kids off at church but to bring them home to it, you need two things: 1) a willingness to fight intruders, and 2) the right weapons with which to fight. This combination is the partnership between the home and the church.

The desire must be in the home, but many of the resources can come from the church. Concerning the scare in our house during the middle of the night, I was willing to fight, but I had nothing with which to protect my family. I need tools to protect my family from more than just external intruders. I need tools to protect my family from the enemy. Church leaders equipping committed parents to disciple their children will accomplish much for the Kingdom and keep the next generation secure. In the fight to protect the home, the church leadership can and should provide the right tools to defend the home.

THE RIGHT EQUIPMENT

To assist parents, ensure you have the right equipment. First, as mentioned before, disciple the parents within your congregation. Grow them up to follow Christ characterized by lives of obedience. Provide them opportunities not just to come to church events and programming, invest in their lives for them to grow up in Christ.

Second, unite the family at church rather than segregate them. The last verse in the Old Testament prophesies concerning the coming of the LORD. "And he will turn the hearts of the fathers to their children and their hearts of children to their fathers, lest I come and strike the land with a decree of utter destruction" (Mal 4:6). The significance of this verse concluding the Old Testament can not be overstated. The coming of Jesus was to usher in a time when families would be reunited. Unfortunately, we are creating church cultures where we do the complete opposite and segregate families as soon as they hit the church campus parking lot.

> Unfortunately, we are creating church cultures where we do the complete opposite and segregate families as soon as they hit the church campus parking lot.

Currently, we are reversing the trend at North Side and putting families back together. We still have age appropriate teaching and programs, but we are also focusing on getting families back together. We recently did away with some children's services so that they could worship alongside their parents. We also removed different types of services so that multigenerational families could worship alongside each other. It has been amazing to see, in some cases, four generations of one family singing God's praises alongside each other. With these changes, our family worship guides have proven to draw these families back together. Whatever your ministry context is, evaluate whether or not your church is currently uniting families or segregating families.

Third, provide periodical training and resources for the parents within your congregation. These types of helps can come in many different forms. Churches can resource parents by highlighting helpful books. Church leadership can provide training on how parents can evangelize their own children. Church leaders can also equip parents by partnering families with ministry organizations in which an entire family can serve together.

In addition to these types of resources, we have also trained parents concerning how to protect their children. We live in a very dangerous environment where many forces are trying to endanger your children. The only problem – walls can't stop these intruders. The rise of media influence is gaining ground by the day. The problem is that most children are smarter with technology than their parents. Most parents are unaware that secret codes are used by teenagers to keep their snooping parents at a distance (ex. CD9 – Code 9 which means parents are around, NIFOC – naked in front of computer, S2R – send to receive pictures, etc.).

With the risk of seeming "uncool" to your children, you must take drastic measures to keep your children safe because other people are taking drastic measures to corrupt your children. Any attempt to provide a fail proof plan to protect your children would be outdated within a week's time, but certain questions can be used to serve as a guide. First, what type of access do your children have to media? Second, how knowledgeable are you concerning the content they are absorbing? Third, what are their friends like? Fourth, who is teaching them "sex ed?" Finally, can you monitor their activity? The very fact that your child would explode if you asked for a password shows the reason you need one. So much of text messages and social networking is done in a private world, what are you doing to monitor what your child is receiving and what your child is producing?

Why is it so important to monitor your child's activity? Because other worldly forces are influencing their worldview. While you can do a fantastic job as a parent teaching your children, you can also lose your child by allowing sinful influences into their lives. You can't keep your child out of the world, but you can, to some extent, keep the world out of your child. When churches can unite parents together to share collective wisdom and biblical guidance through these types of training events, multiple homes will reap the rewarding benefits.

REALITY TELEVISION

One of the greatest ways to equip parents is to expose them to what other parents around them are doing. By sharing the stories of families within one's own congregation, other parents can be "stimulated to love and good deeds" (Heb 10:24) that can be practiced in their own homes. During our "Legacy" series at North Side, I recorded four "Home Invasion" videos. In our Sunday morning worship services, I showed an edited video of my "invasion" of a church member's home from earlier that week. I arrived at the home with a film crew and interviewed an entire family about a particular faith aspect prevalent in their home. This was North Side's reality television show in the truest sense.

I chose the four families based upon a specific activity that I already knew the family practiced. I had heard of these practices through my relationship with them or due to their leadership within the church. The casual setting allowed for church members to see inside of other members' homes concerning how these families practically made Christ the center of their homes.

The first family had three sons under the age of 3. At dinner time, one of the boys reaches in a box beside the kitchen table and selects a Christmas card with a family on it in order to pray for that specific family before supper. This creative way to pray kept the family prayers from getting stagnate and kept the family engaged with the needs of those around them. When I asked the parents' goal in their child rearing, they stated that their job is to make disciples.

The second family highlighted the conversion experiences of their two elementary-aged children. This family placed a "Re-Birth Certificate" in each of the boys' rooms, and the parents annually celebrate the boys' "re-birthdays" in order to reiterate their earlier decisions.

These celebrations reminded the family of those decisions and renewed the joy of their salvation (Ps 51:12). While the parents evangelized their oldest son, that son eventually led his younger brother to Christ.

The third family I interviewed had recently adopted a boy from Guatemala. Even after birthing their three biological children, this family desired to disciple another child who was less fortunate. While the parents readily admitted that the adoption process and the following challenges were difficult, they knew that God who led them to adopt this boy would equip them to evangelize their son. While it is obvious from appearance that something is different with this family, each encounter opens the door for the family to share the gospel.

The fourth family highlighted had taken their two teenage boys on a family mission trip to Brazil years ago. While financial circumstances were an obstacle, this family trusted God and experienced amazing events on the mission field together, and their home was never quite the same after their return. Deciding not to vacate that summer but spread the gospel together as a family created a memory and a focus for the family that never alluded them. Due to these parents' initiation, these teenagers were leaders in the church who were reaching out to others themselves.

Throughout all these videos, church members saw parental intentionality as key to the child rearing process. These testimonial videos made a strong impact on the congregation since these families were already practicing what we were preaching during our Sunday services. Through comments given in the "Making Faith Stick" class we offered and stories shared through community groups, many people told me that these videos challenged them in a way that no other element had. These videos provided tangible examples of leaving a godly legacy.

"YOU MIGHT BE NEXT"

At the conclusion of these videos, I would often say, "Thanks for joining us for another edition of Home Invasion, and get ready, you might be next." While the line would normally produce giggles and glances between spouses, it also caused us all to think. If a camera crew came and set up shop in our home, what would they find? Whether or not the film was graciously edited, would we be proud of the content that they captured?

While none of these homes were perfect, they were seeing success concerning family discipleship. The common denominator in all of these homes was this: they were at least trying *something*. Each of these homes were very different in their approaches. The fathers were all very different. The mothers were all very different. The makeup of the children were all very different from family to family. The family dynamics were different, but they were at least trying. They were active. They were intentional. They were doing *something*.

> The common denominator in all of these homes was this: they were at least trying *something*.

And so should you. Your family is unique (that's probably an understatement!). God has shaped you differently than the other families down the block.

Embrace who you are but try something. Evangelize and disciple the people in your home.

At the culmination of our first training emphasis at North Side, we had a baptism service on the front steps of the church sanctuary. Many parents had been active in evangelizing their children, and God had been faithful in saving many precious children. Our pastor had baptized numerous people that evening before he stepped to the side to make room for another baptizer. Another man walked up behind the baptistry and guided a young boy into the waters. This man is not on the church staff. He does not have a clergy license. He has never sat in a seminary class, but he did lead this young boy to Jesus.

When I was asked by an onlooker next to me, "Why is Pastor Jeff not baptizing that boy?"

I looked at my friend and replied, "Because Pastor Jeff is not that boy's primary spiritual leader. His father is."

I will never forget that moment as a minister or as a father. I watched this father lead his son into the baptismal waters and performed the most meaningful baptism I had ever seen. "Son, I am so proud of you. I can't think of a higher honor that I will ever have then being able to be alongside you the other night when you received Jesus. That was the greatest decision you will ever make. I love you more than you could know. It is an unbelievable honor to baptize you, my son, in the name of the Father, the Son, and the Holy Spirit."

I couldn't help but fast forward years down the road in that moment. I prayed for the day when I would have the honor to baptize my own children. I also rejoiced for my new brother-in-the faith.

I thought about how his life would change from this moment forward. If there ever comes a day when he looks back over the photo albums in his family's living room, he will look at a picture that truly says a thousand words. It will reveal a teary-eyed father who had given more for that son than he will truly comprehend until he has is own children. The photo will display the upward glance of a young son looking up to his father physically and spiritually right before he experiences his baptism. This picture reveals that this father took God's commands seriously and poured everything he had into his son. If ever this son doubts his faith or struggles with personal unholiness, I know who he will go to first. He will go to his spiritual mentor: his father.

What could happen if I took God's commands seriously? What if I decided to evangelize and disciple the children in my home? While the specifics are uncertain, I am sure of a few things. If I intentionally mentor my children, they will have a greater opportunity to impact the world a step ahead of me than when I entered the ministry. If I intentionally provide ways for them to serve in ministry contexts, I will allow them to develop a heart and a passion for dedicated service. If I lovingly confront their character or shortcomings, I will provide a training ground for their discipleship. If I allow them to take the lead in family discipleship times, their initial meager attempts will turn into seasoned powerful offerings to God.

To serve truly within my home, I must maintain intentionality. Change doesn't happen in the home by accident, we must decide to make our families a priority. Knowing that the most critical spiritual environment is the one in which they live, I want to provide a home where Christ is unashamedly the center. I refuse to drop my kids off at church — I will bring them home to it.

APPENDICES
RESOURCES TO EQUIP YOUR HOME AND YOUR CHURCH

APPENDIX 1
MINISTRY OUTLINE

This appendix reports the process implemented to equip parents to evangelize their children at North Side Baptist Church. After a thorough study of the biblical mandate and a survey of current effective child evangelism models, I created a strategy to equip parents. Through this process, I experienced greater validation for the model of pastors equipping the saints for the work of the ministry (Eph 4:12).

In December 2007, I preached a message at North Side entitled "The Family Talk" that served as the catalyst for this entire project. In that message, I explained the need for parents to assume the responsibility of primary evangelists and disciple-makers of their children. Many parents responded positively to this message, but other parents were discouraged due to the overwhelming need present in their home. I received some negative responses from parents who had not served as primary evangelists to their now adult children. Other parents, either at a disadvantage due to their home dynamic or due to their lack of confidence in their own abilities, stated child evangelism was not something they felt they could do. As I began this project, I remembered the responses I received and tried to focus my process on encouraging and equipping parents regardless of how previously committed they had been to this process.

DEVELOPING THE DESIRE

Before learning the essentials needed to evangelize their children, the parents at North Side Baptist Church first had to possess a deep desire to assume that biblical role. They had to understand the need before they would assume their biblical responsibility. The first step in this process was to convince parents that they needed to be intentional about their children's spiritual development and they could not rely on anyone else to do their job.

In week one, I published an article in North Side's *Compass* magazine entitled, "Making Faith Stick." In this article, I posted some of the reasoning behind this project, such as dropout rates for college students raised in church, the incompleteness of children's ministry apart from parental training, and the misplaced priorities of Christian parents who emphasize other areas of a child's life over faith. This article also previewed the teaching emphasis for the upcoming months. The piece encouraged parents to spend the following three months intentionally focused on retaining and applying the forthcoming information and training. Through this article, I explained to parents that North Side was going to train them in the necessary elements of the gospel and the practical ways to share that information with their children.

ROADS TO HEAVEN

In order for North Side's members to grasp firmly the message of the gospel, I began a sermon series entitled "Crossroads" that pitted Christianity's message against the messages of Judaism and Islam. I chose these three religions due to their association with Abraham the patriarch and the need to decipher among these three religions theologically. North Side's senior pastor had desired me to teach a sermon series on world religions due to my teaching at the local university in that field. As I began to develop this project, I felt that a great way to help people grasp the message of the gospel was to reveal its uniqueness compared to other religions. The pastor and I collaborated and planned the churchwide teaching emphasis to support the vision of this project.

In that first week, I planned the content of the "Crossroads" series (Appendix 2) and also planned the following two series in detail. Serving as the worship pastor of North Side, I was not going to preach all fifteen messages during the time frame of this project, but I was responsible for the overview, series outline, Scripture passages, and corresponding applications for every message during this period. I also provided the structure and emphasis for the fifteen weeks of small group curriculum and daily devotional guides for the entire church (Appendix 3). Using the *Compass* magazine, North Side stays focused on one big idea a week. After the message each Sunday, the small group curriculum and daily devotionals supported the big idea presented from the pulpit. During this project, I guided the entire discipleship process.

The "Crossroads" series intended to expose false roads to heaven. In the first week, the message focused on "The Jewish Faith." The patriarch Abraham believed, and God stated that he was "justified by faith" (Gen 15:6). Belief leading to salvation has always been God's original plan. Abraham was justified by faith before God had given the Law, and Christians are still justified solely by faith (Eph 2:8-9).

In week two, the message centered upon "The Muslim Salvation." Through revealing the way Muslims regard salvation based upon good works, I presented a sharp contrast to biblical salvation. While works serve as evidence of Christian salvation, the gospel does not require good works to obtain salvation like the Muslim worldview.

In week three, I preached an apologetic message entitled, "The Messiah Tension." The content of the message centered around major objections to Christianity, such as Jesus was good, but he wasn't God. The intent of this message was to reveal the credibility behind the person and message of Jesus so that the congregation could start the upcoming gospel series with proper understanding concerning the exclusivity of Christianity.

During the "Crossorads" series, many members in the congregation openly indicated that their personal view of salvation was challenged. Without knowing the exact terminology of "syncretism," many members acknowledged realization that they had allowed other views of salvation to distort the gospel of Jesus in their minds. Works-based salvation had crept into many people's theology without their realizing the subtle yet dangerous shift. "Crossroads" set up the upcoming "GRACE" series to present the beauty of the gospel against the backdrop of man's attempt to reach God presented in other worldviews.

THE RESEARCH

During "Crossroads," I assembled a focus group of parents. Because this project focused on equipping parents of elementary-aged children, I intended to have the group comprised of parents in the same stage of life. As I prayed over which parents to gather for this team, three couples kept coming to mind. These three couples were currently leading their home to be the primary environments in which their children were evangelized and discipled. Uniquely, one couple had pre-elementary aged children, one couple had elementary aged children, and the other couple had post-elementary aged children. I decided to use these three couples since they already agreed with the vision of this project. Due to their unique situations, I hoped that their interaction based upon their experience would aid older couples in the group mentoring younger couples as they shared what they had learned along the way.

In week two, I contacted the three couples and asked them to pray for a week concerning joining this focus group. During week three, each couple agreed to participate in the focus group. Upon their acceptance,

I mailed them a copy of this project's previous chapters in order to acclimate themselves to the research and the planned methodology for the project. I asked them to read the material over the next few weeks, pray for the families at North Side, and write down any ideas they had concerning how to equip other parents.

Another component for the initial phase of this project was the parent survey. In week four of the project, I formatted the parent survey in preparation for dispersion the following week. This survey collected information concerning a person's knowledge of the gospel and view of the parental role. Due to the size of North Side, I did not hand out a survey to everyone on a Sunday morning. In our church's context, that surveyed information could have changed from week to week. I gave surveys to North Side's community group leaders and Sunday school teachers. Each leader dispersed them to his/her respective group and returned them to the church office.

Working with a team of volunteers and staff members, we collected the data through an online survey site. Some members filled out surveys on paper, and others contributed online. The team put all of the information on paper into the online database and processed the findings (Appendix 9).

While the findings proved to be helpful for sermon development, another benefit emerged. Because some of the survey's questions challenged some members, community groups turned the discussion to some of the questions concerning the gospel and parenting. After the surveys were collected, community group leaders taught biblically concerning these issues. Many groups discussed their answers of questions concerning the role of baptism, an age of accountability, and parental involvement in child evangelism. Not only were the questions addressed through this lay leadership, but these conversations also served to create a greater desire for the upcoming emphases.

PROVIDING THE CONTENT

In the second stage of this project, my intention was to equip the congregation with tools necessary to share the gospel. After this stage, I planned to teach concerning evangelism specifically for children, but at this time, I focused on making sure our members knew the basic contents of the gospel. Due to North Side's varying spiritual backgrounds, the congregation is comprised of seasoned evangelists to fairly new seekers.

The project was scheduled so that the crux of the gospel series would occur on Easter Sunday. As the "GRACE" series began, North Side was informed that the upcoming emphasis' purpose was twofold: (1) to examine oneself to ensure whether one is truly in the faith (2 Cor 13:5), and (2) to share one's faith with someone else (1 Thess 2:8). This second phase was critical in order to equip parents with helpful information in order to evangelize their own children in the next stage.

THE GRACE SERIES

Using the GRACE tract outline, I designed the sermon material and discipleship curriculum (Appendix 4) to spend one week on each letter of the acrostic for the word "grace" (God, Rebellion, Atonement, Conversion, Eternal Life). The "GRACE" church emphasis began at the beginning of week 4 of this project as the church studied the holiness of God. In week 5, the emphasis focused on the sinfulness of all people and the punishment for sin. The Sunday before Easter, North Side studied the atonement and celebrated communion in all of the services at the beginning of week 6. Easter Sunday started week 7 of this project as the congregation focused on conversion. In week eight, we concluded the "GRACE" series with the topic of eternity. At the beginning of each message, I made sure that the preacher spent time reviewing the information the church had learned the previous weeks.

Throughout the services leading up to Easter, I incorporated intercessory prayer for the lost in Greenwood during the services. A prayer leader focused the congregation on praying for specific people that they knew personally who needed the gospel. North Side incorporated prayer cards in which each member prayed for three specific people during the weeks leading up to Easter, hoping those people would respond positively to the gospel. Through these prayer times, we continued to encourage prayer for one's children if they had not yet received the gospel.

During week 6, I also began a midweek prayer service for the church. I invited members to forfeit their lunch break on Wednesdays for a time to pray and to fast for different emphases. On different weeks, we prayed specifically for the lost, the families of the church, and specifically for parents to evangelize their children. During this time, the church staff and other committed members gathered to pray for the salvation of those needing the gospel.

Throughout the "GRACE" series, North Side experienced over forty conversions. Many of the conversions were older adults. In each week, we gave an opportunity for people to become Christian, and North Side experienced conversions every week during this series. During this series, we baptized someone each week as well. In this phase of the project, the purpose was for parents to understand the gospel. Before parents could evangelize their children, I needed to make sure that parents themselves were saved and fully understood the gospel message.

In community group discussion, leaders were encouraged to allow members to practice sharing the "GRACE" outline with each other. In my own community group, I saw men grow in their ability to share the gospel each time we practiced. From recent converts to seasoned Christians, many members indicated a firmer grasp on the content of the gospel and showed greater confidence in their ability to share that information with another.

FOCUS GROUP FINDINGS

During week 5 (second week of "GRACE"), I assembled the focus group for the first meeting. They brought helpful insights into the project's findings, such as how their parents were involved in their own spiritual development, how they had seen successes and failures in their own home, and what type of training had prepared them to become evangelists. While these parents did confirm their passion for evangelizing their own children, they also did not deny fear associated with their own inabilities. They easily empathized with parents who felt unqualified for the job, but these parents were not shrinking back from their responsibility. Their insight into the fears of most parents proved to be helpful as I crafted the upcoming "Legacy" series. As the first meeting concluded, I gave them a focus group questionnaire (Appendix 5) and asked them to complete it before we reconvened the following week.

The three couples, my wife, and I gathered together during week 6 to discuss our answers to the provided questions. Out of the 8 people in this group, only 1 person was converted in the presence of her parents. While this member was thankful for the experience, she vividly remembered that she was doing more of the questioning, and her parents really never took any initiative with her concerning faith conversations.

While the degree of parental involvement varied from person to person, all group members wished their parents would have been more intentional with their spirituality. Many of the stories involved a parent's taking the child to church but never displaying a personal devotion for the child to observe. Certain group members indicated that their parents encouraged moral behavior apart from the biblical reasoning behind morality.

Through the remaining discussion, key items emerged. First, the parents were concerned they were going to force Christianity on their children. Since their own parents had not been intentional enough, these parents were worried they might overemphasize obedience to the Lord so much that it would cause their children to rebel into prodigal status. Interestingly, no one in that group said that his or her own parents did enough, but they had always heard people warn about not forcing religion on their children. In this group's knowledge, they had never encountered someone who had walked away from the faith due to authentic followers of Jesus who had been intentional with their children. They could count many people who walked away from the church whose story was a home led by parents devoted to religious institutions, but whose home was devoid of any significant change. Church attendance minus real change resulted in straying children. Consistent followers of Jesus typically produced another generation of consistent followers of Jesus.

Second, the uniqueness of each child within a home was noted. One father of post-elementary aged children noted that he had raised all three of his children in the same manner, and each of them was displaying differing levels of Christian devotion. Due to this discussion, I noted that it is important for parents not only to study the gospel, but also to study intently the individual child they are evangelizing. A packaged presentation will not succeed equally with each child. A parent must study his or her child to know how to present the gospel uniquely since each child's needs and understanding are unique, but a wise parent will make the most of every opportunity presented with that child (Col 4:6).

During this time, I was also heavily involved in the development of two parent councils. This project served as a catalyst on our staff to start having conversations concerning ministry strategies to children. We knew we must equip parents, but we also needed to evaluate our current ministry practices to ensure our strategy was assisting parents. One group focused on children's ministry while the other group focused on student ministry. These groups of parents gathered together to evaluate current ministry practices and to plan for future development. As I worked with these groups of parents, I pushed for ministry models that focused on assisting parents as they evangelized and discipled their children.

PREPARING THE EVANGELISTS

Through the first two stages of this project, I had presented North Side with the need for the gospel and the content of the gospel. For this third section, I focused on equipping parents to deliver the message of the gospel to their children. While North Side had experienced great success in corporate evangelism efforts in the previous weeks, the focus turned to commissioning parents onto the mission field within their own homes.

In order to prepare evangelists, I planned on using two components: (1) the "Legacy" church wide teaching series (Appendix 6), and (2) the "Making Faith Stick" course (Appendix 7). Chapter 2 of this project provided the preaching and community group content for the "Legacy" series in utilizing five of the six passages exegeted. Chapter 3 provided the content for the "Making Faith Stick" class. The intent was that the messages on Sunday mornings, the community group curriculum, and the personal devotional material would mobilize parents of elementary aged children to come to the four-week course. During the weeks leading up to this series and during this series, I worked with the children's ministry director to develop children's curriculum that focused on the message of the gospel and the need to obey parents.

THE LEGACY SERIES

The "Legacy" series started on week 10 of this project. As with the previous two series, I was responsible for providing the message content, service development, community group focus, and personal devotional material. As we intentionally develop content for the entire week around one big idea, we strive to make services united around one central idea. During "Legacy," I put extra attention into every song selection, video element, and announcement that went into these services. By the time each sermon started, the message of the day had already begun.

On the first Sunday of the series (week 10 of the project), I preached a message entitled "Your Kids' Best Chance" from Deuteronomy 6:4-9, highlighting the need for parental involvement in a child's spiritual development. I explained that the most critical spiritual environment is the one in which one lives, and each parent needed to ensure that his or her children were encouraged spiritually in the home. This message connected the content of the previous series to the practical steps of the current series in order to make changes within homes.

In week 11, my senior pastor preached "A Family's Decision" from Joshua 24, mobilizing family members to decide to make God the center of the home.

As the invitation to this message, I led a family worship song I wrote, titled "Your Home" and inspired by this passage. On that Sunday, we encouraged families to make the decision to declare their homes as God's home.

I preached a message entitled "Generational Hand-Me-Downs" during week 12. This message from Psalm 78 encouraged parents and grandparents to teach the Bible and their individual testimonies within their homes. The example in Psalm 78 reveals parents teaching children their own missteps with God in order that the children will not follow the same path.

In week 13, I preached a message entitled "Disciplining and Discipling" from Ephesians 6:1-4. While this message addressed all family members, I primarily focused on the pivotal role of fathers in the spiritual development of their children. In this message, I also instructed children on their biblical role to honor their parents.

My pastor preached the final message on week 14 entitled "A Less Than Ideal Home" from 2 Timothy 1:4-7. The goal of the message was to encourage single parents or those parents without a supportive partner to persevere. With so many families in this situation, my pastor provided hope for those parents who felt isolated.

HOME INVASION

During "Legacy," I recorded four "Home Invasion" videos. From week 11 to week 14, I showed an edited video on Sunday mornings of my "invasion" of a church member's home. I arrived at the home with a film crew and interviewed an entire family about a particular faith aspect prevalent in their home. I chose the four families based upon a specific activity that I already knew the family practiced. I had heard of these practices through my relationship with them or due to their leadership within the church. The casual setting allowed for church members to see inside of other members' homes concerning how these families practically made Christ the center of their homes.

The first family had three sons under the age of 3. At dinner time, one of the boys reaches in a box beside the kitchen table and selects a Christmas card with a family on it in order to pray for that specific family before supper. When I asked the parents' goal in their child rearing, they stated that their job is to make disciples.

The second family highlighted the conversion experiences of their two elementary-aged children. This family placed a "Re-Birth Certificate" in each of the boys' rooms, and the parents annually celebrate the boys' "re-birthdays" in order to reiterate their earlier decisions. While the parents evangelized their oldest son, that son eventually led his younger brother to Christ.

The third family I interviewed had recently adopted a boy from Guatemala. Even after birthing their three biological children, this family desired to disciple another child who was less fortunate. While the parents readily admitted that the adoption process and following challengers were difficult, they knew that God who led them to adopt this boy would equip them to evangelize their son.

The fourth family highlighted had taken their two teenage boys on a family mission trip to Brazil years ago. While financial circumstances were an obstacle, this family trusted God and experienced amazing events on the mission field together, and their home was never quite the same after their return. Due to these parents' initiation, these teenagers were leaders in the church who were reaching out to others themselves.

Throughout all these videos, church members saw parental intentionality as key to the child rearing process. These testimonial videos made a strong impact on the congregation since these families were already practicing what we were preaching during our Sunday services. Through comments given in the "Making Faith Stick" class and stories shared through community groups, many people told me that these videos challenged them in a way that no other element had. These videos provided tangible examples of leaving a godly legacy.

MAKING FAITH STICK

One of the main goals of the "Legacy" series was to motivate parents of elementary-aged children to attend the four-week course, "Making Faith Stick" (Appendix 7). I started the class on the Wednesday after the second sermon in the "Legacy" series. Since North Side's primary means of discipleship is community groups, I decided to teach two sections of the course on the two times when most parents attend community groups. On week 11, I started the Wednesday night section and repeated the course on Sunday nights starting during week 12. Between the two sections, over 100 parents attended the course.

In the first week of the course, I focused on teaching gospel essentials. I reviewed the curriculum taught in the "GRACE" series. During this first session, I made attendees share the gospel and their testimony with a partner. While this endeavor was uncomfortable for many, I reiterated the need for each person's confidence in communicating this information with his or her children.

Each week of the course, I assigned specific homework sections for the parents. The homework for week 1 consisted of two major assignments. First, each parent was encouraged to share his or her personal testimony with the children in the following week in order to let them see the parent's genuine conversion. Second, each parent was assigned to recruit and equip prayer partners who would intentionally pray for the salvation of those particular children.

The following week, I personally received prayer cards from two couples attending the class. One couple sent us a picture of their two girls with five specific prayer requests concerning their salvation. I received the other prayer cards at a wedding reception when two members, both with children of their own from a previous marriage, were marrying each other. As a keepsake, this couple gave each attendee a frame with prayer requests for their children's salvation and their responsibility as parents. In addition to these two examples, I heard many other testimonies of parents who recruited prayer partners for their children.

During week 2 of the course, I focused the content on learning levels. I provided each parent with biblical concepts concerning God, Jesus, the Holy Spirit, salvation, and others that children should be able to understand at certain ages. I also taught on the sensitive subject of an age of accountability. I explained that while the term "age of accountability" is not in the Bible, God's Word does indicate that children are secure up to a certain level of spiritual understanding (for more details, see Appendix 7).

During this session, I divided the group into smaller groups according to their children's ages. In these groups, the parents talked through as many biblical concepts on the list according to their children's ages, and they shared ideas and helpful tips to communicate these truths. One parent attempted to illustrate the Trinity for his six year old by revealing that he is a husband, father, and worker all at the same time – just as God has always been the Father, the Son, and the Holy Spirit. Another parent shared how she used discipline moments to reveal why her child desperately needed Jesus.

In week 3 of the course, I taught the first part of the evangelistic steps using the acrostic "CHILD." I taught parents to teach the Bible *chronologically* [C], *highlight* teachable moments [H], and *initiate* open-ended questions [I]. While I assigned homework in each prior session, this week had specific homework instructions for each of these three major sections. I emphasized the need for parents to develop some type of plan for biblical education within the home since, without parental intentionality, the process rarely occurs.

In the final week of "Making Faith Stick" (starting on week 14 of the project), I taught the final two evangelistic steps: *live* an authentic example [L] and *decipher* a child's readiness [D]. I encouraged parents to develop a strategy concerning how to reach each child upon deciphering each child's readiness or a lack thereof. These steps ("CHILD") provided opportunities to communicate the gospel ("GRACE") to their children.

During these weeks, I also posted blog articles to answer questions that I did not have enough time to address from the pulpit or in the class. I had received questions over the phone or through email concerning topics regarding the family. One such question was posed by a parent who felt hopeless because she had not provided a godly home for her children, and she did not know what to do since they were adults now. These posts not only served as a way to answer legitimate questions, but I also provided links to resources for parents who wanted to study further.

BAPTISM CELEBRATION

Due to the number of conversions North Side experienced during the "GRACE" series, many people awaited baptism. I scheduled an outdoor baptism event during week 15 of this project in order to celebrate God's work in our midst. Leading up to that week, recent converts had been baptized on Sunday morning, but many adults and children were still waiting to be baptized.

The staff contacted all recent converts and invited them to be baptized on a Sunday night on the front lawn of the church. Once they agreed, we encouraged them to invite friends and family members to their baptism. I designed an "evite" on North Side's website where a person could email people an invitation to his or her upcoming baptism celebration. This invitation provided details about the upcoming baptism service and allowed the person to write a personal message to the recipients.

Using a portable baptistry, our staff set up a baptism event on the front steps of the worship center facing the main road. Different staff members baptized individuals that they had led to Christ. The final baptism was the highlight of the evening as a non-ordained father baptized his son. This father had led his son to Christ, and he desired to baptize him as well. This emotional moment for this father served as a great conclusion to this project but an even better beginning for things to come at North Side. After the baptisms concluded, North Side's church body enjoyed a time of fellowship to celebrate all that God had done over the past few months. During the time of this project, 15 children were baptized.

EVALUATION PROCESS

During week 15 of the project, I evaluated the project with the help of other members. The goal of collecting this information was not only to provide feedback for this project, but also to develop a long-term strategy for equipping parents to evangelize their children. I did not want to see this emphasis as an isolated event but rather an ongoing strategy of the church.

The first group of evaluations came from the parents who attended the "Making Faith Stick" course. Through a simple six-question survey, they shared what information helped them the most (Appendix 8). No attendee stated that he or she was hoping to learn something that the course did not cover. Most parents indicated that the course was helpful and the homework, when applied, worked well in their homes. In order to equip more parents, many attendees indicated that they would like to see the curriculum recorded on video for individual or small group training or printed in some format.

I also received evaluation from the original focus group that I met with at the beginning of this project. I sent them a packet containing all the curriculum used and asked them to fill out a survey evaluating the entire project. I asked what they believed that parents now understood as a result of this project, and all families indicated that the members of North Side are more equipped to share the gospel and to assume responsibility for the evangelism and discipleship of the children in their homes. While these families had been involved in training sessions in these areas in the past, they indicated that they never felt such confidence in their personal ability to evangelize. They also indicated a need to train parents in this material periodically.

Through the process of implementing this project at North Side Baptist Church, I became overwhelmed at the great need for equipping parents. While I consider North Side a spiritually healthy congregation, this process revealed how North Side has failed to equip parents for their biblical responsibilities. I rejoice in what took place over these fifteen weeks, but this process called my attention to the work that is still left to do.

At the end of this project, many of North Side's members do have a better understanding of the gospel and further accept parental responsibility concerning child evangelism. Over 100 parents have been trained to share the gospel with their elementary-aged children. The following chapter will evaluate the whole process and examine how to equip parents even further.

THEOLOGICAL REFLECTIONS

As I began this project, I believed in the centrality of the home concerning the evangelism and discipleship of one's children, but the further I delved in this subject matter, the more I discovered the importance of this biblical concept. Not only should parents evangelize their children because of the biblical mandate, but that dynamic also has the greatest chance of success and the greatest hope to leave a godly legacy. God's call is for Christians to love him and then model that love for the following generations to witness (Deut 6:4-9).

As a result of this project, I also desire a restructuring of children's and student ministry at North Side Baptist Church. The only ministry noted in the Bible concerning evangelism to children is parents evangelizing their own children. Any church ministry that expects parents only to support their efforts as the church evangelizes their children has already begun with unhealthy pretenses. Because of this shift, I believe that I need to help lead children's and student ministries to focus on equipping and assisting parents to evangelize their children and not vice versa.

The specific role of fathers throughout this theological study challenged me greatly. The biblical mandate for male leadership concerning spiritual matters in the home (Eph 6:4) is a stark contrast with what many Christian homes experience. God spoke repeatedly throughout the pages of Scripture to motivate men to lead in the home. Male reluctance to lead started in the Garden of Eden when Adam passively took of the forbidden fruit from the hands of his wife (Gen 3:6). Part of sin's curse on women for this act would be their desire to lead over their husbands (Gen 3:16).

In homes and churches, men must realize that God calls them to lead. The passivity of men is causing many homes and churches to become endangered. Due to men's reluctance to lead, women feel the need to step into the void. In order to revive Christian homes, men are going to have to assume the mantle of spiritual leadership. Where they are lacking, they must commit to seek help for improvement.

Another essential theological element I discovered through this project was the call for pastors to equip the saints for the work of ministry (Eph 4:12). When ministers and church ministries wrongfully assume sole responsibility for evangelizing children in their church, they are robbing parents of the joy associated with accepting their biblical role as evangelists.

Parents do not know how to evangelize their children primarily because pastors have failed to equip them. Through this process, I have renewed my belief in the role of pastors equipping members for ministry. As a minister, my job is not to do the work of the ministry, but it is to equip the members in the congregation to do the work of the ministry themselves. Through this initiative, evangelistic numbers are not merely added; they are multiplied. Ministers must equip their congregations to evangelize their children. They must equip fathers to lead spiritually in the home. They must equip mothers to support the father's leadership, and they must equip children to obey their parents as they lead.

Throughout this process, I have been reminded of the grace of God and his power to transform families. Regardless of a church's or a family's past, God is capable to bring about authentic life change. The American church has allowed generations to go missing because of neglecting the mandate for parents. This neglect will have effects for a few generations, but for those willing to lead homes biblically, many generations behind them will reap the benefits (Exodus 20:6).

PERSONAL REFLECTIONS

Personally, I grew greatly through this process. I experienced personal growth due to the level of preparation needed to teach this material. In the past, I have experienced the pressure of weekly teaching deadlines. Attempting to work in sermon preparation time during the week with other ministerial duties is a challenging task that all ministers encounter.

Due to the extensive amount of time I spent exegeting the passages from which I would preach, when the delivery time came, I was more than well prepared. During this project, I often had too much material to teach concerning a passage and had to learn to prioritize the most important information. When I taught during this project, I experienced a humble confidence concerning how I handled the biblical texts and the subject matter. The number of hours spent in study not only provided plenty of information to teach, but that preparation time also gave me an even greater credibility in sharing with the congregation.

During this project, I also learned the lesson as a minister to utilize many different ways to teach a congregation. While some learned most during a sermon, others benefitted from a testimonial video. Through audio, video, publications, and other elements, I was reminded that different type of learners within a congregation call for different types of teaching.

By providing different ways for people to learn, I heard from a number of people commenting that they had benefitted from the content in different ways. If I had relied solely on Sunday morning messages to deliver the content, some people might not have attained the growth they experienced through small groups, personal devotions, or other methods. The effort exerted to teach this subject matter made me rethink the way we teach the church as a whole through every spiritual emphasis.

Finally, engulfing myself in the study of the family made me a better husband and father. Due to the content I was learning, I often prolonged finishing certain elements of the project because my family had to take priority. If I become a successful minister and lose my family in the process, I have failed as a man of God. While many people rightfully lament flagrant moral failures of ministers, I also developed a disdain for an unhealthy busy ministerial career.

As a minister, it is easy to get caught in the trap of focusing on pure numerical church growth, but this project has helped me to define success differently. Possibly, my greatest efforts in the kingdom of God in my lifetime are how I evangelize and disciple my children. If I completely invest myself in their spiritual lives, they will be trained to do more for the kingdom than their father ever did. I am thankful for how this project equipped North Side Baptist Church, but I eagerly anticipate the fruit of this work to impact many generations of my own family.

CONCLUSION

My attempts to equip parents to become evangelists at North Side Baptist Church have been fruitful and rewarding. In any type of ministry, it is difficult to determine success. By the response of positive feedback and the stories of parents implementing the material in their homes, I am grateful to share that God has blessed this process.

The rewarding part of this process has been the application within homes. While any minister loves hearing positive feedback concerning the delivery of a message, something special happens when a minister hears that lives are being changed by the truth he has proclaimed. Through personal testimonies I have heard, I have honestly seen a change in the church concerning beliefs and practice pertaining to the centrality of the home.

While the exact specifics of this ministry project might not be repeated in certain ministry contexts, I am confident that most churches need at least to re-evaluate the process of child evangelism and the commitment for equipping parents. For the sake of the children in every church, leaders must wrestle with the difficult task of equipping parents to evangelize their children. I pray that church leaders everywhere will leave the type of godly legacy in their homes and in their churches that brings immense glory to Jesus.

APPENDIX 2
CROSSROADS OUTLINE

SERIES DESCRIPTION

Three of the major world religions all claim the same source of beginning. Judaism, Christianity, and Islam all hold Abraham to be the man from whom their religion began, but all three of these religions arrive at a dramatic crossroads at the person of Jesus Christ. The message, ministry, and life of Christ forever separated these movements. The "Crossroads" series educated the congregation concerning the differences of these three religions and come to a resolution at the person of Jesus.

WEEK 1: THE JEWISH FAITH

God chose Abraham to be the father of his nation. Before the Law was ever mentioned, God declared Abraham righteous according to his faith. Unfortunately, Judaism has turned into a religion based on keeping God's approval by doing good works, and they missed the coming Messiah in the person of Jesus. This week, I explained the life of Abraham, especially highlighting the passages associated with God's promises such as Gen 12:1-3. Through this study, I explained the nature of God's nation and his original plan for salvation through faith which has never changed since the beginning.

WEEK 2: THE MUSLIM SALVATION

In the 600s AD, a businessman named Muhammad emerged from meditating in a cave and claimed to have received a message from God. Over the years of receiving revelations, his theology would develop into claiming that his way was the original way from God and that Judaism and Christianity were not a way to God. In the message, I spent a portion studying the life of Muhammad. From this angle, I preached from Eph 2:1-10 revealing how the message of Jesus' grace and peace goes against the message of works and forced conversion espoused by Islam.

WEEK 3: THE MESSIAH TENSION

Throughout the Old Testament, the prophets were very specific in describing the coming Messiah. While Jews claim the Messiah has not yet arrived and Muslims claim Jesus was only a mere prophet, every person must deal with the fact that the person of Jesus fulfilled every single prophecy written about the Messiah hundreds of years before his birth. Through this week's message, I revealed how Jesus clearly fulfilled the prophecies of the Messiah. and how the world has never been the same since. Each person must answer, like Peter, Jesus' question concerning, "But who do you say that I am?" (Matt 16:13-20).

APPENDIX 3
PROJECT DEVOTIONAL GUIDE

Throughout this project, I provided daily biblical readings and weekly small group guides to correspond with the weekly message. I have listed the devotional passages below. The small group study focused on these daily readings.

I. Crossroads
   A. Week 1: Abraham and Judaism
      1. March 2: Abram's (Abraham's) Origin - Gen 11:26-32
      2. March 3: God Calls Abram - Gen 12:1-9
      3. March 4: God's Covenant with Abraham - Gen 15:1-6
      4. March 5: Abraham's Faith Commended - Heb 11:8-19

    5. March 6: Abraham's Actions Proved His Faith - Jas 2:21-24
    6. Memory Verse: Gen 15:1
  B. Week 2: Muhammad and Islam
    1. March 9: Abraham, Sarah, and Hagar - Gen 16:1-4
    2. March 10: Sarah and Hagar - Gen 16:5-15
    3. March 11: Hagar and Ishmael are Sent Away - Gen 21:8-21
    4. March 12: Ishmael's Descendents - Gen 25:12-18
    5. March 13: Ishmael's and Issac's Spiritual Legacies - Gal 4:21-31
    6. Memory Verse: Gal 4:28
  C. Week 3: Jesus and Christianity
    1. March 16: Jesus is God in the Flesh - John 1:1-14
    2. March 17: Jesus is the Promised One - Matt 26:57-68
    3. March 18: Jesus Taught About the Kingdom of God - Matt 5:1-20
    4. March 19: Jesus Took Our Death Penalty - Rom 5:1-11
    5. March 20: Jesus Rose from the Dead - Matt 28:1-10
    6. Memory Verse: John 3:16
II. GRACE
  A. Week 4: GRACE Begins with God
    1. March 23: God is Spirit - John 4:1-26
    2. March 24: God Created Everything - Gen 1:1-25
    3. March 25: God is Holy - 1 Tim 6:13-16

    4. March 26: God is Love - 1 John 4:7-21
    5. March 27: God Made Man in His Image - Gen 1:26-31
    6. Memory Verse: 1 John 4:10
  B. Week 5: Rebellion from GRACE
    1. March 30: Our Sins Separate Us From Our Creator - Isa 59:1-8
    2. March 31: All People Are Sinners - Rom 3:1-23
    3. April 1: Sin Makes Us Enemies of God - Jas 4:1-6
    4. April 2: Sin Brings Death - Rom 6:19-23
    5. April 3: Sin is Darkness - 1 John 1:5-10
    6. Memory Verse: Rom 3:23
  C. Week 6: GRACE Atonement
    1. April 6: One Died for All - 2 Cor 5:14-21
    2. April 7: God Made Us Alive in Christ - Eph 2:1-9
    3. April 8: Jesus Was Made Like Us So He Could Take Our Place - Heb 2:9-18
    4. April 9: Jesus Predicts His Own Sacrificial Death - John 12:23-30
    5. April 10: Christ Died for Us - Rom 5:1-9
    6. Memory Verse: Rom 5:8
  D. Week 7: Conversion of GRACE
    1. April 13: God Saves Us By His Grace - Eph 2:1-10
    2. April 14: A Jailer's Life is Changed - Acts 16:16-34
    3. April 15: Peter Tells the Jews to Repent and Turn to God - Acts 3:12-26
    4. April 16: God's Grace Gives Direction to Our Lives - Titus 2:11-15

5. April 17: Jesus is the Only Way - John 14:1-14
6. Memory Verse: Rom 6:23
E. Week 8: Eternity from GRACE
1. April 20: Whoever Hears the Word and Believes Has Life - John 5:16-24
2. April 21: Whoever Believes is Not Condemned - John 3:10-17
3. April 22: Eternal Life is Knowing God Through Jesus - John 17:1-5
4. April 23: Jesus Brings New Life - 2 Cor 5:11-21
5. April 24: Jesus Brings Real Life - John 10:1-10
6. Memory Verse: John 5:24

III. Legacy
A. Week 10: Your Kids' Best Chance
1. May 4: Teach the Children, Part 1 - Deut 6:1-13
2. May 5: Teach the Children, Part 2 - Deut 6:14-25
3. May 6: Spiritual Lessons - Ps 34
4. May 7: Trusting and Not Rebelling - Ps 78:1-11
5. May 8: Fathers Neglecting Their Children - Luke 1:5-17
6. Memory Verse: Deut 7:9
B. Week 11: A Family's Choice
1. May 11: Choosing Life or Death - Deut 30:11-20
2. May 12: A Dramatic Contest - 1 Kgs 18:16-40
3. May 13: Choosing to Live by God's Word - Ps 119:17-32
4. May 14: Choosing the Best - Luke 10:38-42

    5. May 15: Moses' Faithful Choices - Heb 11:24-28

    6. Memory Verse: Josh 24:15

  C. Week 12: Generational Hand-Me-Downs

    1. May 18: Tell the Next Generation - Ps 78:1-8

    2. May 19: Teach All the Time - Deut 11:1-21

    3. May 20: Children Must Hear the Word - Deut 31:1-12

    4. May 21: Children Need to Hear What God Has Done for Us - Luke 8:26-39

    5. May 22: Cornelius: A Good Example - Acts 10:1-8

    6. Memory Verse: Prov 22:6

  D. Week 13: Disciplining and Discipling

    1. May 25: Lessons for Life - Ps 34:11-22

    2. May 26: Children are Valuable - Psalm 127

    3. May 27: Pay Attention to Spiritual Things - Eccl 12:1-7

    4. May 28: Children are Important to Jesus - Matt 19:13-14

    5. May 29: Instructions for Christian Homes - Col 3:18-25

    6. Memory Verse: Prov 20:11

  E. Week 14: A Less Than Ideal Home

    1. June 1: Faithful Influence - 2 Tim 1:2-7

    2. June 2: Faithful to Share What God Has Done - Gen 21:1-7

    3. June 3: Faithfully Making a Request of God - 1 Sam 1:1-20

    4. June 4: Faithful in Unusual Circumstances - Luke 1:26-38

5. June 5: Faithful Even Though in a Minority - Acts 10:1-8
6. Memory Verse: 2 Tim 1:14

APPENDIX 4
GRACE OUTLINE

SERIES DESCRIPTION

"Gospel" is a word used a lot in church. What does it really mean? Using the acronym "GRACE," this series looked at God's good news and its meaning for every person.

WEEK 4: GOD OF GRACE

The gospel begins with God. Oftentimes, people look at creation and believe that God made it solely for people to enjoy. As Creator, God created for his glory and his pleasure. In Col 1:15-20, Paul explains that everything – including people – were made by God and for God. If God made people, he also has the divine right to tell people how to live. Gospel, grace, and salvation are all wrapped up in the holiness of God.

WEEK 5: REBELLION FROM GRACE

The holy, Creator God has put the knowledge of the divine in every person. In Rom 1:18-25, Paul described that all humans were without excuse due to God's revealing of himself. Unfortunately, every person took that knowledge and still chose to rebel against God. God's holiness was met with man's rebellion, and grace was needed to repair that relationship.

WEEK 6: ATONEMENT OF GRACE

Since mankind rebelled against God's holiness, Jesus came to redeem a fallen world and reconcile the people to the holy God. In Mark 14:22-26, Jesus took the Lord's Supper and explained the coming sacrifice that he would make. His death on the cross would provide a way to repair man's broken relationship with God due to sin. The grace of Jesus led him to sacrifice himself for the sake of mankind.

WEEK 7: CONVERSION OF GRACE

In Rom 4:1-8, Paul explained that some of Israel's key figures could not attain righteousness by works. Even before the Law came into being, God reconciled people according to his grace. A person is converted when they understand that salvation is a complete work o f God's grace. This message encouraged hearers to confess and believe in the gospel of Jesus Christ.

WEEK 8: ETERNITY OF GRACE

In John 3:31-36, Jesus promised that the ones believing in him would have eternal life. The gospel does not only have effects in this life but in the hereafter. Once a person is transformed by this gospel of grace, that person can experience abundant life now and a secure eternal life in heaven with Jesus.

APPENDIX 5
FOCUS GROUP QUESTIONNAIRE

Listed below is the focus group questionnaire that I gave to a small group of parents at the beginning of the project. I listed some of the answers below each question in bullet form.

QUESTIONS

1. Who led you to salvation through faith in Christ?
    a. "My childhood pastor."
    b. "My youth minister."
    c. "A friend in college."

2. If your parents did not lead you to Christ, what role did they play in your salvation?
    a. "My parents took me to church, but I never saw tangible faith in their lives."
    b. "I wish my parents would have done more. I asked questions as a child about faith, but they

seemed to brush it off at home. I had to get my questions answered at church."

c. "My parents would talk about God to a certain extent, but if it got too heavy, they told me to ask the preacher."

3. What issue concerning personal evangelism of your child do you feel most ill-equipped?

a. "I am not sure when they are truly ready to become Christians."

b. "I am fearful that I am going to push too hard, and they reject Christianity."

c. "I'm afraid I might leave something out in my description of the gospel, and they not get a complete picture."

4. What questions do you think your child might ask you concerning salvation in which you would not have a confident answer?

a. "I feel I could answer most any question they ask me."

b. "I don't know how to explain to them why people of other religions aren't going to heaven."

c. "I'm afraid of him asking about the Trinity."

5. What do you think that your child currently understands about salvation?

a. "Each of my children understands differently, and we raised them all the same way. The better behaving child doubts his salvation, and my hellion is sure he is saved."

b. "I think he understands enough to be saved, but I want to make sure that I am sure about what is enough."

c. "Our children knows that God exists, but they don't seem to understand the weight of disobeying him just yet."

APPENDIX 6
LEGACY OUTLINE

SERIES DESCRIPTION

Every parent will leave a legacy to their children. But are you really leaving the type of legacy you want them to have? Statistics are reporting that somewhere between 70-88% of church kids are not active in church by the end of their freshmen year of college. This decline comes at a time when more churches have more activities for children and students than ever before. So maybe the problem isn't that the church doesn't have enough programming for children, but maybe God's design is that a child's best chance at following God is the child's parents being intentional about their spiritual development. Are you ready to leave a legacy?

WEEK 10: YOUR KIDS' BEST CHANCE

At the cusp of entering the Promised Land, Moses gathered the people of Israel for one last list of instructions. Before reminding the people of the commands God had given them, Moses reminds the people that the most important thing they could do was to love God extremely. In Deut. 6:4-9, Moses tells the people to love God with all their heart, soul, and strength, but he then tells them to model and teach that love to their own children. From the beginning, God orchestrated family in such a way that a child's best chance at following God is the model and instruction he or she receives from his or her parents.

WEEK 11: A FAMILY'S CHOICE

After Joshua had led Israel through military victories in order to regain the Promised Land, Joshua turns back like Moses to instruct the people one last time. At this juncture, he understands that he cannot speak for an entire nation, but he can speak for his family. Joshua decides that regardless of what his culture and his country does, he is going to lead his family to serve the Lord. In Josh. 24:14-18, Joshua makes his declaration for his house to follow God. Have you made that declaration?

WEEK 12: GENERATIONAL HAND-ME DOWNS

In Ps. 78:1-8, the psalmist informs parents to pass down instruction concerning the Lord to the coming generations. While the psalmist reminds the people of their constant faithlessness in light of God's faithfulness, he pleads that the parents should teach their children the nation's past mistakes in hope that they will not be repeated. Children do learn about God from instruction within the church, but their greatest chance of learning is within the home. Even if parents do not feel qualified, God has given them a responsibility to inform children concerning God's work recorded in the Bible and God's work within their own lives.

WEEK 13: DISCIPLINING AND DISCIPLING

In Eph. 6:1-4, Paul gives some clear instructions for children and parents. He reminds children that their submission to their parents is understood to be obedience to God. While Paul commands children to obey both their fathers and mothers, he specifically instructs fathers to take the lead within the home concerning a child's disciplining and discipling. Paul informs fathers of their God-give responsibility to raise their children according to God's principles.

WEEK 14: A LESS-THAN-IDEAL HOME

If an ideal home is one in which the father leads the way for the children's spiritual development, our culture is in trouble due to the current state of families. With the increase of single-parent homes, what is the answer for children who start their spiritual journey at a disadvantage? The pastor Timothy grew up in a home with a father who did not follow God, but his mother and grandmother had genuine contagious faith. As Paul wrote to him in 2 Tim. 1:3-7, he provided encouragement for parents who are not in the ideal situation. Even if one's home isn't the way that it should be does not mean that God can't make it that way.

APPENDIX 7
MAKING FAITH STICK OUTLINE

The "Making Faith Stick" course lasted four weeks. With each lesson, I provided homework for parents to complete before the following week. The outline of the curriculum is below.

WEEK 1 - GOSPEL ESSENTIALS

In this first of four sessions of "Making Faith Stick," we are going to focus on the gospel essentials. What is essential that your child must understand in order to respond to the gospel?

I. Your Child's Greatest Need: Your child's greatest need is the gospel.
    A. Concerns
        1. What if I don't present the information correctly?

        2. Wouldn't a trained professional be more trustworthy?

        3. What if I turn them off to Christianity?

    B. Benefits

        1. Children remember what is intentionally celebrated.

        2. Parents are the most constant figure in a child's life.

        3. It is God's ideal evangelistic model.

II. God's Greatest News: God's greatest news is his gospel of GRACE (Eph 2:8-9).

    A. God

        1. It's all about God (Rev 4:11).

        2. Since he created all things, he has the right and power to be Lord over all things (Col 1:16).

        3. Alongside God's great holiness, we also recognize his great love for us (Ps 8:3-4).

    B. Rebellion

        1. We messed it up (Rom 3:23).

        2. Our sins have causes us to be separated from the Holy God (Isa 59:2).

        3. God's punishment for sin is death (Rom 6:23).

    C. Atonement

        1. Atonement means to repair a broken relationship.

        2. Through Jesus' life, he lived sinless in obedience to God (Heb 4:15).

        3. Through his death, he became a substitute for our punishment (Rom 5:8).

    4. Through his resurrection, he defeated death and provided eternal life (1 Cor 15:55).
  D. Conversion
    1. Jesus is the way (John 14:6).
    2. To become a Christian, we must willfully trust in Jesus alone for salvation (Acts 4:12).
    3. To repent means to turn from our sins in order to turn to Jesus in obedience (Luke 13:3).
    4. God's gift of salvation is a free gift of grace (Rom 6:23).
  E. Eternity
    1. We're going home (John 5:24).
    2. Jesus is able to give sinners new life (2 Cor 5:17).
    3. Your salvation is only as secure as the hands that hold it (John 10:28).

III. Your Greatest Story: Your greatest story that you will ever tell your children is how Jesus saved you
  A. What was your life like before Christ?
  B. What happened at conversion?
  C. What has your life been like after Christ?

IV. Homework
  A. Recruit family prayer partners.
  B. Find a way to share your story with your children this week.

WEEK 2 - LEARNING LEVELS

In this second of four sessions of "Making Faith Stick," we are going to focus on the learning levels. What is your child able to comprehend about faith at his or her age?

I. Age of Accountability: The Bible does not provide precise descriptive information concerning an age of accountability.
    A. Origin of the Idea
        1. The need for an age of accountability arose from the concept of original sin (Ps 51:6).
        2. The commonly held belief is that God would not condemn a child who had died before that child had the ability to respond to the gospel.
        3. King David believed that he would see his baby who had died (2 Sam 12:23).
    B. Problems Concerning Deciphering the "Age"
        1. In Matt 18:2, Jesus esteemed a child as the greatest in the Kingdom, so children obviously can become Christian.
        2. Paul told Timothy "that from childhood you have known the sacred Scriptures, which are able to instruct you for salvation through faith in Christ Jesus" (2 Tim 3:15).
        3. The early church retained no records of allowing young children to be baptized for at least the first two centuries of its existence.
        4. Children of the same age are not at the same maturity level.

C. Theories
   1. School systems hold that six years of age is when children should begin their formal education.
   2. Whenever a child begins to indicate interest in matters concerning God, the time is right regardless of age.
   3. A child is ready when that child not only understands when he or she has done something wrong, but when that child is able to understand the consequences of sinful actions.
   4. Statistics show that a large majority of children become a Christian between the ages of six and eight.
   5. Parents must find the balance of showing concern over a child's spirituality without pressuring the child's decision.

II. Progressive Levels: Each child is unique concerning what they can comprehend and when they can comprehend it; five key areas to teach your child are God's Identity, God's Activity, Your Relationship, Your Identity, and Your Activity.
   A. 0-4 Years
   B. 5-6 Years
   C. 7-9 Years
   D. 10-12 Years

III. Homework
   A. Evaluate your child's knowledge corresponding with the appropriate learning levels.
   B. Explain GRACE to your child.

WEEK 3 - EVANGELISTIC STEPS (PART 1)

In this third of four sessions of "Making Faith Stick," we are going to focus on the first evangelistic steps. What parental practices are working?

I. "CHILD" Evangelistic Steps: A survey of effective children ministry reveals that there are recurring steps that parents can take to evangelize their children. To help remember, we will use the acrostic "CHILD."
   A. Chronologically Teach the Bible
   B. Highlight Teachable Moments
   C. Initiate Open-Ended Questions
   D. Live an Authentic Example
   E. Decipher a Child's Readiness

II. The Steps
   A. Chronologically Teach the Bible
     1. The Big Problem
       a. Most Christians do not understand the overarching story of the Bible.
       b. Teaching children solely stories removed from context does not provide them with an understanding of the one big story.
       c. Can you place these stories in chronological order?
          1) Moses leading Israel out of Egypt
          2) Jonah and the fish
          3) Jesus turns water into wine
          4) Joseph sold into slavery by brothers
          5) Saul on the Damascus Road
          6) Abraham's sacrifice of Issac
          7) David vs. Goliath
          8) John the Baptist's beheading

        9) Ezra and Nehemiah rebuilding Jerusalem

        10) Joshua and Caleb spy out the land

    d. Isolated stories can teach moral lessons and not God's truth.

  2. The Big Picture

    a. Creation - It's all about God

    b. Fall - We messed it up

    c. Promise - God wants to help

    d. Incarnation - Jesus came for us

    e. Example - Taught us how to live

    f. Redemption - Jesus is the way

    g. Worship - Living to please him

    h. Community - We need each other

    i. Missions - Others need him

    j. Eternity - We're going home

B. Highlight Teachable Moments

  1. Questions

    a. Statistics say that by the time a child becomes fifteen years old, that one child has asked perhaps half a million questions.

    b. While parents may become annoyed by all the questions beginning with what, when, why, where, and how, intentional parents will use these opportunities to steer the conversations toward God.

  2. Events

    a. Intentional

        1) Parents can create teachable moments through certain events.

        2) What kind of events can you create to develop a teachable moment?

  b. Unintentional
    1) As a child experiences life, God opens doors for parents to turn conversations toward faith issues.
    2) What kind of events happen during the day that you could turn into a teachable moment?
 3. Sinful Behavior
  a. When a child sins, a mindful parent will use that opportunity to explain the spiritual ramifications for what just transpired versus simply punishing the child.
  b. Parents must remember that even through discipline, they are to have the gospel as their focus.

C. Initiate Open-Ended Questions
 1. The Dangerous Alternative
  a. Understanding that children are able to remember stories and retain phrases well at an early age, parents must be careful that children are understanding the gospel and not simply regurgitating the message.
  b. In an attempt to gain parental or peer approval, some children may appear desirous of conversion.
  c. Parents must refrain from using leading or closed questions.
  d. If a parent asks a child, "Do you believe Jesus died on the cross for you?" that child's positive response gives little indication of actual comprehension.
 2. The Effective Question

a. What a child has to answer with more than a simple word or repeat a common phrase, a parent will be able to grasp that child's real comprehension of spiritual matters.
    b. To avoid leading question, parents should initiate open-ended questions which better reveal a child's understanding.
  3. The Special Meeting
    a. If a chid prompts a conversation with a parent concerning spiritual matters, that parent should respond in such a manner that the child sees that parent's motivation and excitement.
    b. A parent could heighten a child's anticipation by telling that child to meet him or her for a special meeting since this talk is so important.
    c. Once the conversation begins, a parent should ask open-ended questions to gauge the child's spiritual awareness.
III. Homework
  A. Make a Bible teaching plan
  B. Highlight a teachable moment within the next day
  C. Initiate open-ended questions to discover where your child is spiritually

WEEK 4: EVANGELISTIC STEPS (PART 2)

In this fourth week, we are going to look at the last two evangelistic steps and review the course material.

I. The Steps
   A. Live an Authentic Example
      1. Reality - How important is my example?
         a. While intentional teaching has a significant impact upon children, studies suggest that the most important element in a child's spiritual development is parents modeling an authentic example of obedience to Christ.
         b. Children are able to ascertain the difference between a parent's desire and a parent's obligation.
         c. It is unreasonable for a parent to believe that a child would possess a type of faith not witnessed within his or her own parents.
         d. Through the example of holy living and the teaching of one's personal faith, a parents is able to show a child that his or her faith is genuine and tangible.
      2. Checkup - What's the status of my example?
         a. Would you be pleased if your child repeated your quiet time habits?
         b. Would you be pleased if your child modeled your prayer life?
         c. Would you be pleased if your child's speech imitated yours?
         d. Would you be pleased if your child's marriage was like your own?
         e. Would you be pleased if your child imitated your sinful habits?
   B. Decipher a Child's Readiness
      1. Beware

a. While a parent may incessantly pray for and tirelessly teach for a child's comprehension of the gospel, that parent must commit never to manipulate his or her children into a forced conversion.

b. Parents must beware of the danger that a child's motivation for becoming a Christian could be because a friend recently became a Christian and got baptized.

c. For a child to be sure concerning his or her salvation, he or she must see this decision as isolated from peer or parental pressure.

2. Investigate

a. If a child returns from church or some event and indicates he or she was converted, the child's parents should ask the child to explain what happened as a way to assess the child's spiritual depth.

b. A parent should not suspect that the decision was illegitimate, but that parent needs to ask questions to reveal whether that moment should be classified as conversion or as a spiritual moment without true life-changing commitment.

c. A tree is known by its fruit (Matt 7:16), and a parent should not preemptively treat a child's decision as though his or her spiritual future is now firmly settled, but neither should that child's desire be belittled.

3. Celebrate

a. If a child does seem confident in his or her salvation, the parent is then responsible for affirming his or her decision and teaching that angels in heaven are actually rejoicing at that moment (Luke 15:10).

b. Once a child has been reborn, parents can help cement the reality of that experience in the mind of a child by celebrating the event.

c. Whether a parent takes that child out to dinner, calls family members with the exciting news, or interviews the child on video to document the experience, a parent can better ensure that this event does not become lost in a plethora of childhood experiences.

d. As a child grows in Christ, a parent should continue to monitor his or her development over the years to reaffirm his or her decision.

II. Home Inspection: What areas need to be addressed?
   A. GRACE
   B. Testimony
   C. CHILD
   D. Resources
III. Homework
   A. Make a family plan.
   B. Check your example.
   C. Decipher your child's readiness.
   D. Celebrate extravagantly.

APPENDIX 8
MAKING FAITH STICK EVALUATION

Listed below are the survey questions given to parents who took the "Making Faith Stick" course. I listed some of the answers below each question in bullet form.

EVALUATION

1. What was the most helpful information you learned from this class?
    a. "Driving home the fact that even after our child accepts Christ, we keep coming back and reminding the child of that decision."
    b. "Evaluating my status then comparing it to what I want for my kids when they are adults."
    c. "The format was good in that you took time speaking on topics and then we were able to discuss with people at our table. Through that

discussion, you could obtain ideas and feel comfortable in that you were not alone."

2. Did you see success through the homework? What did you do and what happened?

   a. "Our kids were not ready for some of it. We need to be more intentional."
   b. "Yes, we talked with grandparents to address specific prayer concerns regarding the children's salvation."
   c. "Revitalized our prayer time with the kids."
   d. "Yes, we got family members to pray for our children, but we also assigned each child to pray for one of the other children."

3. What do you wish you would have learned but it wasn't covered?

   a. "How to get through to a defiant child."
   b. "Talk more about how to play catch up - like if you have older kids but haven't laid a great framework so far."
   c. "Maybe some brainstorming and sharing with other concerning disciplining techniques and more emphasis on teachable moments with examples."

4. As a result of this class, what did you change/improve in the home?

   a. "I am going to be a better example for my child. I want him to see my faith at work more – reading the Bible in front of him, etc."
   b. "I'm more aware of how important being intentional is. I can't just sail through and deal with things as they come up. I have to be proactive and anticipate as well as lead. Hard

to do!"

c. "My spouse and I became a team in order to develop an evangelistic plan for our children."

5. How would you recommend North Side help equip parents on an ongoing basis?

a. "Provide a periodical newsletter with some of this material highlighted."

b. "Align children's teaching with the adult's sermon series."

c. "Would it be possible for you to set up four-week blocks that you could be available for a community group to reserve you to teach this to their group? You could go more in-depth and have more discussion this way."

6. Should this material be expanded for a resource available to parents? What type of resource would be most helpful?

a. "Make it into a Bible study DVD."

b. "A family devotional book would be helpful."

c. "A notebook and DVD, kind of like Beth Moore Bible studies. You could watch a video and do the worksheets. This could be used if a community group wanted to do it together."

d. "Offer it on videos on the website."

APPENDIX 9
PROJECT GOALS

This project intended to accomplish five goals essential to the success of equipping parents to evangelize their children at North Side Baptist Church, Greenwood, South Carolina. The first goal was to teach parents the necessary elements of the gospel. Before a parent could adequately present the gospel to his or her children, this parent had to be completely comfortable with the essentials of the gospel message. Many parents usher their children to their pastor to evangelize their children because they fearfully believe that they may not sufficiently present the information. Parents rightfully dread presenting a misunderstood gospel due to the accompanying eternal severity, but their fear should not keep them from accepting their biblical responsibility. To ensure success in this task, parents must be confident in the gospel message not only for their own salvation, but also for the salvation of their children. The leadership of any church must take responsibility to regularly teach parents the message of the gospel.

The second goal was that the parents understand the stages of salvation. Once the gospel message is taught to parents, a church's leadership must then educate parents concerning what happens in a person when he or she is converted. Many parents assume that a prayer shared with a pastor and a baptism service in a church are the proof needed for a child's conversion. If a parent is going to have a pivotal role in his or her child's conversion, then that parent must comprehend the different stages of conversion. Parents need to understand what God's role is concerning salvation and what their child's role is concerning salvation. Baptism needs to be understood as an act of obedience as a Christian and not a prerequisite for salvation. Parents also need to understand their child's conversion as a starting point for sanctification and not a finishing line for salvation.

The third goal was that each parent in the congregation understand that his or her biblical responsibility was to become the primary evangelist in his or her children's lives. As seminaries have increasingly produced and churches have more often staffed more age-specialized ministers such as youth pastors or children ministers, Christian parents have begun to believe that they need to trust the Christian professionals to take care of their God-given responsibility. Parents no longer need to attempt to share the gospel with their children because they have ministers in their church to do that job. While additional evangelists in a child's life are definitely a welcomed presence, no church staff member's evangelistic training can ever compare with the impact of a parent's concerned and concentrated efforts to tell a child the gospel. Upon the examination of Scripture, parents will understand that they are to be their children's primary evangelists because that role is what God has commanded of them

The fourth goal was that the parents in our congregation develop the skills to share the gospel effectively in relationship to the individual child's comprehension levels. Once a parent understands theologically the elements of the gospel, the stages of salvation, and the biblical role of the parent, the church must equip parents to share the gospel intentionally with their children. Because every child is at a unique comprehension level, parents must be given the resources to gauge their child's ability to understand the gospel. In the process of evangelizing children, two dangers arise. First, some parents might preemptively proclaim their child's conversion when that child is not at an age or at a comprehension level to truly understand. Second, some parents might wait too long to address salvation waiting for a day in the future when their children can understand fully. Through this project's equipping parents with helpful information and practices, the goal was for parents to find an effective approach to sharing the gospel with their children. The goal was to also equip the parents with creative ways to bring gospel conversations into everyday life in the home.

The final goal was that as a minister and as a father, I would personally improve in my ability to share the gospel with my own child. Through my research, my prayer was that my children will eternally benefit due to a father who rightfully assumes his God-given mantle of primary evangelist in his home. While I can teach my children many lessons during their time as they grow up, I pray that I personally reflect the biblical role to make Christ the center of our home. I desire too much the blessed privilege to walk with my children across the threshold of conversion to allow someone else to take that responsibility away from me. As I progressed through this research, I prayed that my heart would increase in love for my children and my skills as an evangelist would improve so that I may share the greatest news with the most precious people in my life.

BIBLIOGRAPHY

BOOKS

Agnew, Travis, and Marissa Mounts. *North Side Baptist Church: The First 40 Years*. Greenwood, SC: n.p., 2007.

Arnold, Bill T. *Encountering the Book of Genesis*. Encountering Biblical Studies. Grand Rapids: Baker Books, 1998.

Baldwin, Joyce G. *The Message of Genesis 12-50: From Abraham to Joseph*. The Bible *Speaks Today*. Leicester, England: InterVarsity Press, 1986.

Barna, George. *Revolutionary Parenting: What the Research Shows Really Works*. Wheaton, IL: BarnaBooks, 2007.

_____. *Transforming Children into Spiritual Champions*. Ventura, CA: Regal, 2003.

Baucham, Voddie. *Family Driven Faith: Doing What It Takes to Raise Sons and Daughters Who Walk with God*. Wheaton, IL: Crossway Books, 2007.

Beougher, Timothy. *GRACE: An Evangelistic Tract*. Louisville: SBTS, 2004.

Boice, James Montgomery. *Joshua*. Grand Rapids: Baker Books, 2005.

Bruce, F. F. *The Epistles to the Colossians, to Philemon, and to the Ephesians*. The New *International Commentary on the New Testament. Grand Rapids: Eerdmans, 1984*.

Bruce, Robert G., and Debra Fulghum Bruce. *Becoming Spiritual Soulmates with Your Child*. Nashville: Broadman and Holman Publishers, 1996.

Butler, Trent C. *Joshua*. Word Biblical Commentary, vol. 7. Waco, TX: Word Books, 1983.

Chall, Sally Leman. *Making God Real to Your Children*. Tarrytown, NY: F. H. Revell *Co., 1991*.

Chapin, Alice Zillman. *Building Your Child's Faith*. Nashville: Thomas Nelson, 1990.

Christensen, Duane L. *Deuteronomy*. Word Biblical Commentary, vol. 6A. Nashville: Nelson, 2001.

Clifford, Richard J. *Psalms 73-150*. Abingdon Old Testament Commentaries. Nashville: Abingdon Press, 2003.

Craigie, Peter C. *The Book of Deuteronomy.* The New International Commentary on the Old Testament. Grand Rapids: Eerdmans, 1976.

Creach, Jerome F. D. *Joshua*. Interpretation. Louisville: Westminster John Knox Press, 2003.

Davies, Margaret. *The Pastoral Epistles*. London: Epworth Press, 1996.

Drescher, John M. *Parents: Passing the Torch of Faith*. Scottdale, PA: Herald Press, *1997.*

Erickson, Millard J. *Christian Theology*. 2nd ed. Grand Rapids: Baker Books, 2003.

Fee, Gordon D., and W. Ward Gasque. *1 and 2 Timothy, Titus*. New International Biblical Commentary, vol. 13. Peabody, MA: Hendrickson Publishers, 1988.

Graustein, Karl, and Mark Jacobsen. *Growing Up Christian*. Phillipsburg, NJ: P&R Publishing, 2005.

Grudem, Wayne. *Systematic Theology: An Introduction to Biblical Doctrine. Grand Rapids: Zondervan, 1994.*

Guthrie, Donald. *The Pastoral Epistles: An Introduction and Commentary*. The Tyndale *New Testament Commentaries. Leicester, England: InterVarsity Press, 1990.*

Halverson, Delia Touchton. *How Do Children Grow? Introducing Children to God, Jesus, the Bible, Prayer, Church*. Nashville: Abingdon Press, 1993,

Hamilton, Victor P. *The Book of Genesis. Chapters 18-50*. The New International *Commentary on the Old Testament. Grand Rapids: Eerdmans, 1995.*

Haystead, Wesley. *Teaching Your Child about God*. Ventura, CA: Regal Books, 1995.

Hess, Richard S. *Joshua: An Introduction and Commentary*. The Tyndale Old Testament *Commentaries*. Leicester, England: InterVarsity Press, 1996.

Howard, David M. *Joshua*. The New American Commentary, vol. 5. Nashville: Broadman and Holman Publishers, 1998.

Hughes, R. Kent, Barbara Hughes, and R. Kent Hughes. *Disciplines of a Godly Family*. Wheaton, IL: Crossway Books, 2004.

Kidner, Derek. *Psalms 73-150*. The Tyndale Old Testament Commentaries. Leicester, England: InterVarsity, 1973.

Koelman, Jacobus, John Vriend, and M. Eugene Osterhaven. *The Duties of Parents*. Classics of Reformed Spirituality. Grand Rapids: Baker Academic, 2003.

Köstenberger, Andreas J., and David W. Jones. *God, Marriage & Family: Rebuilding the Biblical Foundation*. Wheaton, IL: Crossway Books, 2004.

Kraus, Hans-Joachim. *Psalms 60-150: A Commentary*. Minneapolis: Augsburg, 1989.

Lawson, Steven J., and Max E. Anders. *Psalms 76-150*. Holman Old Testament Commentary, vol. 12. Nashville: Broadman and Holman, 2006.

Lea, Thomas D., and Hayne P. Griffin. *1, 2 Timothy, Titus*. The New American Commentary, vol. 34. Nashville: Broadman Press, 1992.

Liefeld, Walter L. *1 & 2 Timothy, Titus: from Biblical Text...to Contemporary Life*. The NIV Application Commentary. Grand Rapids: Zondervan, 1999.

Lincoln, Andrew T. *Ephesians*. Word Biblical Commentary, vol. 42. Dallas: Word Books, 1990.

Luccock, George N. *The Home God Meant*. New York: The Book Stall, 1922.

Mathews, K. A. *Genesis 11:27-50:26*. The New American Commentary, vol. 1B. Nashville: Broadman and Holman, 2005.

McIntosh, Doug, and Max E. Anders. *Deuteronomy*. Holman Reference. Nashville: Broadman and Holman, 2002.

McRaney, Will, Jr. *The Art of Personal Evangelism: Sharing Jesus in a Changing Culture*. Nashville: Broadman and Holman, 2003.

Merrill, Eugene H. *Deuteronomy*. The New American Commentary, vol. 4. Nashville: Broadman and Holman, 1994.

Metzger, Will. *Tell the Truth: The Whole Gospel to the Whole Person by Whole People : A Training Manual on the Message and Methods of God-Centered Witnessing*. Downers Grove, IL: InterVarsity Press, 1981.

Miller, Sue, and David Stall. *Making Your Children's Ministry the Best Hour of Every Kid's Week*. Grand Rapids: Zondervan, 2004.

Mounce, William. *Pastoral Epistles*. Word Biblical Commentary, vol. 46. Nashville: Nelson, 2000.

Neff, Blake J., and Donald Ratcliff. *Handbook of Family Religious Education*. Birmingham, AL: Religious Education Press, 1995.

Oden, Thomas. *First and Second Timothy and Titus*. Interpretation. Atlanta: John Knox *Press, 1989.*

Osborne, Rick. *Talking to Your Children about God*. San Francisco: Harper, 1998.

Phillips, Benny, and Sheree Phillips. *Raising Kids Who Hunger for God*. Tarrytown, NY: Chosen Books, 1991.

Phillips, John. *Exploring the Pastoral Epistles: An Expository Commentary.* Grand Rapids: Kregal, 2004.

Rhodes, Ron. *What Your Child Needs to Know about God*. Eugene, OR: Harvest House Publishers, 1997.

Sears, William. *Christian Parenting and Child Care*. Nashville: Nelson, 1991.

Shelley, Marshall. *Keeping Your Kids Christian: A Candid Look at One of the Greatest Challenges Parents Face*. Ann Arbor, MI: Vine Books, 1990.

Snodgrass, Klyne. *Ephesians: from Text...to Contemporary Life*. The NIV Application *Commentary. Grand Rapids: Zondervan, 1996.*

Spurgeon, Charles, and Roy Clarke. *The Treasury of David.* Nashville: Nelson, 1997.

Stetzer, Ed, and Mike Dodson. *Comeback Churches: How 300 Churches Turned around and Yours Can Too*. Nashville: Broadman and Holman, 2007.

Tate, Marvin E. *Psalms 51-100.* Word Biblical Commentary, vol. 20. Dallas: Word, 1990.

Towner, Philip H. *The Letters to Timothy and Titus*. The New International Commentary on the New Testament. Grand Rapids: Eerdmans, 2006.

Trent, John T., Rick Osborne, and Kurt D. Bruner. *Parents' Guide to the Spiritual Growth of Children*. Wheaton, IL: Tyndale House Publishers, 2000.

Tripp, Tedd. *Shepherding a Child's Heart*. Wapwallopen, PA: Shepherd Press, 1995.

Vos, Howard Frederic. *Genesis*. Chicago: Moody Press, 1982.

Waltke, Bruce K., and Cathi J. Fredricks. *Genesis: A Commentary.* Grand Rapids: Zondervan, 2001.

Walton, John H. *Genesis: from Biblical Text ... to Contemporary Life*. The NIV Application Commentary. Grand Rapids: Zondervan, 2001.

Wenham, Gordon J. *Genesis. 16-50*. Word Biblical Commentary, vol. 2. Dallas: Word Books, 1994.
Whitney, Donald. *Family Worship: In the Bible, in History and in Your Home*. Shepherdsville, KY: The Center of Biblical Spirituality, 2005.

Woudstra, Marten H. *The Book of Joshua*. New International Commentary on the Old Testament. Grand Rapids: Eerdmans, 1981.

Wright, Christopher J. H. *Deuteronomy*. New International Biblical Commentary, vol. 4. Peabody, MA: Hendrickson Publishers, 1996.

Youngblood, Ronald F. *The Book of Genesis: An Introductory Commentary*. Grand *Rapids: Baker Book House, 1991.*

ARTICLES

Bugg, Charles B. "Joshua 24:14-18–The Choice." *Review and Expositor* 95, no. 2 (1998): 279-84.

Draper, James T. "The Ground of All Truth: Deut. 6:4-9." *Faith and Mission* 15, no. 2 (1998): 53-62.

Hayes, Edward L. "Evangelism of Children." *Bibliotheca Sacra* 132, no. 527 (1975): 250-64.

Kennedy, John W. "The 4-14 Window: New Push on Child Evangelism Targets the Crucial Early Years." *Christianity Today* 48, no. 7 (2004): 53.

Nelson, C. Ellis. "Spiritual Formation: A Family Matter." *Journal of Family Ministry* 20, no. 3 (2006): 13-27.

Ngan, Lai Ling Elizabeth. "A Teaching Outline for the Book of Joshua." *Review and Expositor* 95, no. 2 (1998): 161-69.

INTERNET MATERIALS

Agnew, Travis. "The History of North Side" [on-line]. Accessed 7 July 2008. Available from http://www.northsidebc.org/about-us/history; Internet.

Kelly, Mark. "LifeWay Research Finds Parents Look Inward Not Upward for Guidance" [on-line]. Accessed 9 September 2011. Available from http://www.lifeway.com/Article/LifeWay-Research-finds-parents-look-inward-not-upward-for-guidance.

Ledbetter, Tammi Reed. "Better Equipped Than Ever But Less Effective" [on-line]. Accessed 9 September 2011. Available from http://www.texanonline.net/special-reports/better-equipped-than-ever-but-less-effective; Internet.

"Outreach Demographic Trends: North Side Baptist Church" [on-line]. Vista, CA: Outreach, Inc., 2006. Available from http://www.outreach.com; Internet.

For more information and resources, visit
travisagnew.org.

Made in the USA
Lexington, KY
09 October 2012